VOA News Plus

Seisuke Yasunami

Richard S. Lavin

音声ファイルのダウンロード／ストリーミング

CD マーク表示がある箇所は、音声を弊社 HP より無料でダウンロード／ストリーミングすることができます。トップページのバナーをクリックし、書籍検索してください。書籍詳細ページに音声ダウンロードアイコンがございますのでそちらから自習用音声としてご活用ください。

https://www.seibido.co.jp

VOA News Plus

Copyright © 2016 by Seisuke Yasunami, Richard S. Lavin

All rights reserved for Japan.
No part of this book may be reproduced in any form
without permission from Seibido Co., Ltd.

はしがき

　本書『VOA News Plus』はたいへん好評でした前書『VOA News Clip Collection』の続編です。主な違いは、前書ではEnglishCentral上に既存の教材からコンテンツを選びましたが、本書ではEnglishCentral上の既存の教材だけでなくそれ以外からもコンテンツとして利用できるようにしたことです。このことにより、各ユニットの本文の語数も多くなり、リスニング力向上だけでなくリーディング力向上を目指す授業でも利用できるようになりました。

　本書は前書同様に㈱成美堂とEnglishCentralとの共同開発で生まれたテキストです。EnglishCentralは動画を用いて学習できるオンラインプログラムですが、語彙やリスニングやスピーキングなどの練習がインタラクティブに行えるのが特徴です。EnglishCentralは個別学習でも利用できるようになっていますが、大学の授業では主にNative Speakerの先生方によってSpeakingやListeningの授業で採用されています。そこで、4技能の育成を目指した総合教材として日本人の先生方にも幅広くご採用頂けるようにとの願いから、Voice of America Newsのコンテンツやその他のコンテンツから学生の皆さんが興味を持って頂けると考えられるものを厳選して、テキストとして出版させて頂くことにしました。

　テキストは、各ユニットのトピックに関するDIALOGUE、内容に係るVOCABULARY、トピックの英語の確認を行うLISTENING、内容把握に関するTRUE OR FALSE?とQUESTION&ANSWERS、本文にある成句を用いるSENTENCE COMPLETION、本文と関連する英文を完成するSUMMARY、連音や日本人が苦手をする音に関するPRONOUNCIATION、リズミカルな発音練習を行うRHYTHMICAL CAHNT、さらに、オンライン上のEnglishCentralを用いた自習コーナーも利用できるような構成となっています。本書に対応したオンライン上のEnglishCentralの学習サイトも利用できるように設定しています。

　本書『VOA News Plus』とEnglishCentralを用いた学習を通して、学生の皆さんが実践的な英語力のスキルアップを図って頂けるよう著者として願っています。

　最後になりますが、この度のデジタルとアナログを融合する企画を提案頂いた㈱成美堂とEnglishCentralの関係者、また、本書の編集・校正・出版などにご尽力頂いた田村栄一氏に対して心より御礼を申し上げます。

2015年10月
安浪誠祐
Richard S. Lavin

EnglishCentralのご案内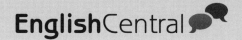

本テキストで学習していただいた動画は、オンライン学習システム「EnglishCentral」で学習することができます。

EnglishCentralでは動画の視聴や単語のディクテーションのほか、動画のセリフを音読し録音すると、コンピュータが発音を判定します。PCのwebだけでなく、スマートフォン、タブレットではアプリでも学習できます。リスニング、スピーキング、語彙力向上のため、ぜひ活用してください。

EnglishCentralの利用にはアカウントとアクセスコードの登録が必要です。登録方法については下記ページにアクセスしてください。

（画像はすべてサンプルで、実際の教材とは異なります）

https://www.seibido.co.jp/englishcentral/pdf/ectextregister.pdf

オンライン版特典動画一覧

Unit 1	1. 宇宙へのメッセージ
	2. NASAが深宇宙の新しい画像を発表
Unit 2	1. 再生医療
	2. 1日で実際に風邪を治す方法
Unit 3	1. 海上保安庁が海で犬を救助
	2. 人間は犬の最高の友達
Unit 4	1. マーク・ザッカーバーグ:「Facebookは急ごしらえで作ったんだ」
	2. デブ・ロイ:言葉の誕生(パート7)
Unit 5	1. 中国がグリーンテクノロジーで先行
	2. 中国とインド:急成長する経済
Unit 6	1. ヴァンダナ・シヴァ:食糧の将来
	2. フード・インク:もうご飯を同じように見られない
Unit 7	1. 騙し絵の町(パート1)
	2. マット・ピーコックがホームレスのためのオペラについて語る
Unit 8	1. インジャスティス: 神々の激突
	2. 義眼でものを見る男
Unit 9	1. 携帯電話で医療
	2. テッドケネディ:「正しくない特権」
Unit 10	1. スティーブン・キング:「博識でなければならない」
	2. 読み方:良い読書レッスンの原則
Unit 11	1. ルワンダのゴリラ・トレッキング
	2. エピック:メアリーと秘密の王国
Unit 12	1. 独創的なニューヨーク市民が竹自転車を開発
	2. 動物の気象予報士
Unit 13	1. 電子工学とコンピュータエンジニアリングの学位をとる
	2. ニコラ・テスラ:天才で発明家
Unit 14	1. 驚くべき宇宙
	2. 宇宙で泣ける?
Unit 15	1. ディズニーのようにかぼちゃをデザイン
	2. スターバックスの注文をラップで

CONTENTS

Unit	Topic	Page
1	**Kimchi in Space** キムチを宇宙へ	1
2	**Is Ginkgo Biloba Effective?** 銀杏は効果的?	7
3	**Our Best Friends Understand Us!** 犬のきもち	13
4	**Gaming Online** オンライン・ゲーム	19
5	**Overtaken by China** 中国に追い越された	25
6	**More Salt with Your Vegetables?** 野菜にもっと塩分を?	31
7	**Homes for the Homeless** ホームレスの人たちへホームを	37
8	**Care for an Exoskeleton?** これからの外骨格	43
9	**Health on the Go** 大忙しの健康	49
10	**E-books Rising** 成長中の電子書籍	55
11	**Health in the Forest** アフリカの森林と薬草	61
12	**Gravity-defying Skateboards** 重力をものともしないスケボー	67
13	**Living Your High-tech Dreams** ハイテクの夢を生かす	73
14	**Onward to Jupiter** 木星を目指す	79
15	**Pumpkins at Halloween** ハロウィンのかぼちゃ	85

UNIT 1

Kimchi in Space

DIALOGUE

▶ 空所に下の語群から適当なものを入れて、英文を完成させなさい。その後、ペアを作って対話の練習をしなさい。　1-02

A: Do you like Korean ¹(　　　　　)?

B: Well, I don't have it very often, so I don't know very many ²(　　　　　). What about you?

A: I love it. I ³(　　　　　) like kimchi.

B: Oh, kimchi. That's fermented cabbage, ⁴(　　　　　)?

> dishes,　especially,　food,　right

VOCABULARY

▶次の語の定義を下から選びなさい。

> 1. understatement (　)　　2. grocery (　)　3. abroad (　)　　4. season (　)
> 5. orbit (　) 6. fermentation (　) 7. bubble (　) 8. dehydrate (　)

(a) a process used in making bread and beer

(b) in or to another country

(c) saying something in an unexaggerated way

(d) to remove water

(e) food

(f) a ball of air or gas

(g) a part (approximately a quarter) of the year

(h) a trip around, e.g., a planet

LISTENING

▶英語を聞いて空所に適語を入れなさい。但し、カッコは内容、下線部は連音に注意しなさい。

fermented 発酵した

take up
[物が空間を]占める、取る

for fear of ～を恐れて

International Space Station
国際宇宙ステーション

Narrator: To say that Koreans love kimchi is to make a startling understatement. The spicy vegetable dish usually ¹_____ fermented cabbage, red peppers, and garlic takes up entire sections of grocery stores.

Traveling businessmen ²(   ) it abroad in their suitcases for fear of doing without.

And any ³_____ history knows that clay pots full of this stuff kept the Korean people ⁴(   ) for centuries during harsh winter seasons.

So, when South Koreans prepared to send astronaut Yi So-yeon to the International Space Station for at least ten days, some asked whether any Korean could ⁵(   ) without kimchi for that long.

Kim Sung-soo is a senior engineer at the Korea Food Research Institute near Seoul. For him, the answer to that question is clear.

Kim Sung-soo: Yi So-yeon will not ⁶(   ) in space without kimchi. Koreans need to eat kimchi every day in order to sustain their health. She'll have all kinds of problems in space without it.

Narrator: But Kim ^{7}_____ taking kimchi into orbit is no simple matter. The dish gets much of its flavor and nutritional value from fermentation. That age-old bacterial process that makes bread rise and gives beer its bubbles can create a series of dangers in a tightly controlled environment of a space voyage.

Kim has ^{8}(   ) most of the last two years in a laboratory making kimchi ready for space.

His team starts by irradiating and slightly cooking regular kimchi to reduce bacteria. Then the dish is frozen and rapidly dehydrated in giant appliances in an industrial facility next door. Finally, it is cut into little cubes that look like biscuits— then, vacuum sealed into plastic bags.

Astronauts can cut ^{9}_____ the bags and add water, rehydrating the cabbage and spices.

Then, it is ^{10}(   ) to eat right out of the plastic.

Kim Sung-soo: Very good.

TRUE OR FALSE?

▶ 内容と合っているものはTを、合っていないものはFを○で囲みなさい。

1. Kimchi is made of lettuce, green peppers, and garlic. [T / F]

2. Kimchi is traditionally kept in steel pots. [T / F]

3. Yi So-yeon is a Korean astronaut. [T / F]

4. Fermentation is a dangerous process in space. [T / F]

5. Kim Sung-soo has spent 12 years finding ways to make kimchi available to astronauts. [T / F]

6. Kim's kimchi is cut into cubes. [T / F]

QUESTIONS AND ANSWERS

▶ 質問の答えを完成した後、ペアを作って、対話の練習をしてみましょう。

(1) A: How popular is kimchi in Korea?

　　B: _____.

(2) A: What did some Koreans worry about when Korea sent an astronaut into space?

　　B: _____.

(3) A: What process accounts for kimchi's flavor and nutritional value?

　　B: _____.

(4) A: In Kim Sung-soo's process, how are bacteria controlled?

　　B: _____.

SENTENCE COMPLETION

▶日本語の意味を表すように、本文から最も適当な語を選んで入れなさい。

1. 北極グマは夏を生き延びるために冬の期間に十分なアザラシを食べる必要がある。
   Polar bears need to eat enough seals during the winter to (　　　) (　　　) (　　　) through the summer.

2. 中年から体重を減らすことは簡単なことではないと栄養士は同意する。
   Nutritionists agree that, from middle age, losing weight is (　　　) (　　　) (　　　).

3. 慢性病の人の多くは毎日の投薬なしにはやっていけない。
   Many people with chronic illnesses cannot (　　　) (　　　) daily medications.

4. アメリカの多くの若者は1日に約5時間はテレビを観たりテレビゲームをやったりして過ごす。
   Many young people in the U.S. (　　　) around five hours a day (　　　) television or (　　　) video games.

5. エッセイを書くとき、概要を書くことから始めるのが良いことがある。
   When writing an essay, it can be useful to (　　　) by (　　　) an outline.

SUMMARY

▶下の語群から最も適当なものを選び、要約文を完成させなさい。但し、英文の文頭に来るものは大文字にしなさい。　1-04

When a Korean astronaut first went into space to ¹(　　　) experiments at the International Space Station, there was ²(　　　) that she would not survive without kimchi. Kim Sung-soo, a ³(　　　) engineer at the Korea Food Research Institute, worked to find a way to ⁴(　　　) kimchi to space travel. Fermenting kimchi in the traditional way would be dangerous on a space ⁵(　　　), so Kim irradiates and cooks it, before freezing and ⁶(　　　) it.

> adapt, concern, conduct, dehydrating, senior, voyage

PRONUNCIATION

▶つなげて発音する音／つながって聞こえる音　　　　　　　　CD 1-05, 06

1語1語、区切って発音するのではなく、つながるように発音します。これをマスターすると自然体で話されている英語が聞きやすくなったり、リズムで発音する時に楽に発音ができます。

次のフレーズを発音してみましょう。

usually <u>made of</u> fermented cabbage　　[meid ɑv] ⇒ [meidəv]メイダヴ
<u>takes up</u> entire sections　　[teiks ʌp] ⇒ [teiksʌp]テイクサプ
carry <u>it abroad</u>　　[it əbrɔːd] ⇒ [itəbrɔːd]イタブロード
any <u>student of</u> history　　[stjuːdnt ɑv] ⇒ [stjuːdntəv]ステューデンタヴ

音声を聞いて、下線部の個所に適語を入れなさい。その後で、自分で発音してみましょう。

1. Any _____ knows that economic booms don't last for ever.

2. This table is _____ local wood.

3. I love playing my guitar, but I'm worried that I won't be able to _____ _____ with me.

4. Those are very useful books. Will you take _____ with you?

5. What is this toy _____?

RHYTHMICAL CHANT

▶下線のところを強調しながら、リズミカルに大きな声で読みなさい。　　CD 1-07

A: <u>Kim</u>chi in <u>space</u>, <u>kim</u>chi in <u>space</u>.
B: <u>That</u> sounds <u>dan</u>gerous, <u>real</u>ly <u>dan</u>gerous.
A: Ir<u>ra</u>diate, <u>freeze</u>, and de<u>hy</u>drate—
　　<u>That's</u> how to <u>bring</u> it <u>safe</u>ly to your <u>plate</u>.

自習コーナー

▶EnglishCentral にアクセスして、『見る』『学ぶ』『話す』『単語クイズ』のタスクを学習してみましょう。

UNIT 2 Is Ginkgo Biloba Effective?

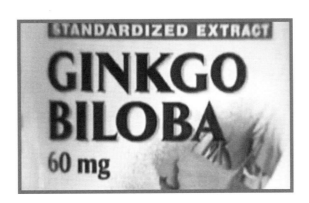

DIALOGUE

▶ 空所に下の語群から適当なものを入れて、英文を完成させなさい。その後、ペアを作って対話の練習をしなさい。　1-08

A: Do you take any ¹(　　　　　)?

B: No, of course not. I don't know anything ²(　　　　　) them. What about you?

A: Well, I take a multivitamin. But most supplements are way too ³(　　　　　).

B: Yes, you can say that ⁴(　　　　　)!

> about,　again,　expensive,　supplements

VOCABULARY

▶ 次の語の定義を下から選びなさい。

> 1. clinical (　) 　 2. aging (　) 　 3. cognitive (　) 　 4. notable (　)
> 5. extract (　) 　 6. symptom (　) 　 7. dementia (　) 　 8. caveat (　)

(a) a warning that something may not be completely true in all cases
(b) to do with the mind
(c) to do with medical treatment
(d) a sign of a medical problem
(e) a substance obtained from a herb, for example
(f) getting old
(g) important or interesting
(h) a disease that interferes with the ability to think and remember

LISTENING

▶ 英語を聞いて空所に適語を入れなさい。但し、カッコは内容、下線部は連音に注意しなさい。

as a means of
〜の手段［方法］として

forthcoming 現れようとしている、すぐに手に入る

so far 今までのところ

cognitive impairment
アルツハイマー病などの認識機能障害

medication 薬物・薬剤［投与］

Narrator: Practitioners of alternative medicine have recommended ginkgo biloba as a means of maintaining and even improving memory among older adults. But until now, strong clinical evidence [1]_____ _____ effectiveness has not been forthcoming.

Doctor Dekosky: This is the first, and so far the only, study that has looked specifically at its ability to [2](_____) decline.

Narrator: For eight years, researchers at six universities across the U.S. studied more than 3,000 adults, [3](_____) 72 to 96, with normal mental functioning or with mild cognitive impairment. Participants received either a 120-milligram dose of ginkgo extract [4]_____ day or a sugar pill.

Researchers found that ginkgo had no [5](_____) effect on memory or attention.

Doctor Dekosky: What we can say is that we find no evidence that ginkgo, over this long period of time, made a difference in whether someone's slow change in memory function, as a function of normal aging, was [6](_____) at all by the medication.

Narrator: Earlier research showed that ginkgo did nothing

for people with symptoms of Alzheimer's disease, nor ⁷_____ help reduce other forms of dementia.

Researchers say this latest study is notable because it was ⁸(   ) with the largest number of participants, and it rules out the herbal supplement as a useful treatment for memory loss.

Doctor Dekosky: We found that there was no effect of the ginkgo biloba on these very slow but clearly detectable changes in thinking function in late life.

Narrator: But the researchers added one caveat: while ginkgo biloba is ⁹_____ in slowing down the mental changes of aging, they say it is safe and has no side ¹⁰(   ).

TRUE OR FALSE?

▶ 内容と合っているものはTを、合っていないものはFを〇で囲みなさい。

1. There is plentiful clinical evidence that ginkgo biloba is effective for maintaining memory. [T / F]

2. Dr. Dekosky's study involved researchers at eight universities. [T / F]

3. People in the control group in the study received sugar pills. [T / F]

4. The study found that ginkgo biloba is effective in treating Alzheimer's disease. [T / F]

5. The study was conducted with a large number of participants. [T / F]

6. Ginkgo biloba is safe. [T / F]

QUESTIONS AND ANSWERS

▶ 質問の答えを完成した後、ペアを作って、対話の練習をしてみましょう。

(1) A: For what purpose have alternative medical practitioners recommended ginkgo biloba?

　　B: _____.

(2) A: What was the purpose of Dr. Dekosky's study?

　　B: _____.

(3) A: How many patients were involved in the study?

　　B: _____.

(4) A: What did earlier research show about ginkgo biloba and dementia?

　　B: _____.

SENTENCE COMPLETION

▶日本語の意味を表すように、本文から最も適当な語を選んで入れなさい。

1. 水泳は一番良い運動として医師によく勧められる。
   Swimming is often (　　　　　) by doctors (　　　) the best form of exercise.

2. 大学生にとって、塾で教えることは収入を補ったり自分の知識を深める手段となる。
   For a university student, teaching at a cram school is a (　　　　) (　　　) (　　　　　) income and deepening one's knowledge.

3. 数千人の人たちがその事故で影響を受けたが、政府の対応はまだない。
   Thousands of people were affected by the accident, but no governmental response (　　　) (　　　) (　　　　　).

4. 選挙のマニフェストで、その政党は歳入不足の問題の解決としての所得税の増税を外した。
   In the election manifesto, the party (　　　　) (　　　) higher income taxes (　　　) solutions to the problem of the deficit.

5. 政府の施策は雇用を増やさなかったが、貧困も減らさなかった。
   The government's measures have not increased employment; (　　　　) (　　　) (　　　　) reduced poverty.

SUMMARY

▶下の語群から最も適当なものを選び、要約文を完成させなさい。但し、英文の文頭に来るものは大文字にしなさい。　1-10

While in many societies modern synthetic medicine has largely ¹(　　　　　) herbal medicine, there is still interest in herbs, which were the ²(　　　　　) of many early synthetic drugs. One herb that has ³(　　　　　) persistent interest is ginkgo biloba, an herb commonly used in Chinese medicine, which is ⁴(　　　　　) to improve blood flow and be effective in many conditions such as ⁵(　　　　　) problems, vertigo, and mental functioning in the elderly. However, a recent study failed to find any ⁶(　　　　　) of an effect for ginkgo biloba.

> attracted, basis, believed, evidence, replaced, vision

PRONUNCIATION

▶日本人にとって発音や聞き取りに難しさを伴う音 [θ][ð]   1-11, 12

[θ] は無声音であるのに対して、[ð] は有声音です。どちらも、上前歯の先と舌で発音される摩擦音で、発音する際に歯と舌の平らな部分が接触しているように注意してください。前者の場合はしっかりと息を出し、後者の場合は、振動が出ていることを確認してください。

次の単語を発音してみましょう。

think [θíŋk] / forthcoming [fɔ́ːθkʌ́miŋ] / synthetic [sinθétik] / health [hélθ]
thousand [θáuznd] / the [ðə] / they [ðéi] / that [ðæt] / without [wiðáut]

音声を聞いて、(　　　) 内に適語を入れなさい。その後で、自分で発音してみましょう。

1. (　　　) said (　　　)(　　　) couldn't live (　　　) music.
2. (　　　) now exist (　　　) of (　　　) drugs.
3. For me (　　　) is (　　　).
4. A (　　　) is (　　　) that is used to measure temperature.
5. Did you understand (　　　)(　　　) of (　　　) play?

RHYTHMICAL CHANT

▶下線のところを強調しながら、リズミカルに大きな声で読みなさい。   1-13

A: A <u>supple</u>ment for <u>cog</u>nitive de<u>cline</u>?
B: <u>Gink</u>go bi<u>lo</u>ba, <u>gink</u>go bi<u>lo</u>ba.
A: <u>Slows</u> de<u>cline</u> in the <u>el</u>derly?
B: <u>Gink</u>go bi<u>lo</u>ba, <u>gink</u>go bi<u>lo</u>ba.
A: <u>How</u> does it <u>work</u>?
B: I <u>really</u> don't <u>know</u>. <u>Maybe</u> it <u>doesn't</u>.
A & B: <u>Gink</u>go bi<u>lo</u>ba, <u>gink</u>go bi<u>lo</u>ba.

自習コーナー

▶EnglishCentral にアクセスして、『見る』『学ぶ』『話す』『単語クイズ』のタスクを学習してみましょう。

UNIT 3

Our Best Friends Understand Us!

DIALOGUE

▶ 空所に下の語群から適当なものを入れて、英文を完成させなさい。その後、ペアを作って対話の練習をしなさい。　1-14

A: Do you have a pet?
B: Yes, we have a cat.
A: A cat? ¹(　　　　　) you find cats a bit ²(　　　　　)?
B: Not ³(　　　　　). I guess you have a dog, do you?
A: Yes, it's a poodle. I enjoy ⁴(　　　　　) with it.

> distant,　playing,　don't,　especially

VOCABULARY

▶ 次の語の定義を下から選びなさい。

> 1. petting (　) 　 2. treat (　) 　 3. MRI (　) 　 4. mechanism (　)
> 5. motionless (　) 　 6. neurological (　) 　 7. similarity (　) 　 8. glimpse (　)

(a) magnetic resonance imaging
(b) an aspect that is almost the same
(c) touching an animal affectionately
(d) related to the nerves and brain
(e) a quick look
(f) the way that something works
(g) without moving
(h) a special food eaten outside regular meal time

LISTENING

▶英語を聞いて空所に適語を入れなさい。但し、カッコは内容、下線部は連音に注意しなさい。

1-15

lab = laboratory 実験室

ELTE University
エトヴェシュ・ロラーンド大学

scan ～をスキャンする、走査する
emotionally
感情的に、情緒的に
whine [犬が] クンクン鳴く

subject 被験者

striking
目立つ、人目を引く、著しい

Narrator: Dogs are not usually ¹(   ) in a lab environment, but, ²_____ _____ little petting and lots of treats, they can be trained to sit still even in an MRI scanner. That's how researchers at Hungary's ELTE University ³_____ to get images of their brains at work.

Research Fellow Attila Andics says it helped them better understand the dogs' relationship with humans.

Attila Andics: We have known for a long time that dogs and humans ⁴(   ) a similar social environment, but now our results show that dogs and humans also have similar brain mechanisms to process social information.

Narrator: After training 11 dogs to stay motionless while their brains were scanned, the researchers checked their neurological responses to about 200 emotionally relevant sounds, from whining and crying to playful barking and laughing. They then ⁵(   ) the responses from human subjects.

They found striking similarities. Andics says it opens new possibilities for research.

Attila Andics: It establishes a foundation ⁶_____ _____ new branch of comparative neuroscience, because until now it was not possible to ⁷(   ) the brain activities of a non-primate and a primate brain in a single experiment.

Narrator: The canine mind is also being studied at Duke University in North Carolina. Co-director of the school's Canine Cognition Center, Evan MacLean, says that the Hungarian results ⁸_____ important step ⁹(   ). MacLean spoke to VOA via Skype.

Evan MacLean: We've known for a long time that dogs have a lot of behavioral similarities compared to humans, but we don't really know anything, or very little at least, about whether some of these behaviors are ¹⁰(   ) similarly inside the brain of the dog, so this research is providing a first glimpse as to whether some of these behavioral similarities are underlied* by similar neural processes.

TRUE OR FALSE?

▶ 内容と合っているものはTを、合っていないものはFを○で囲みなさい。

1. Researchers at ELTE University examined dogs' brains using an MRI scanner. [T / F]

2. The researchers played sounds such as crying and laughing to the dogs. [T / F]

3. The researchers found that humans' and dogs' brain mechanisms are totally different. [T / F]

4. Attila Andics says that their study opens up new possibilities in neuroscience. [T / F]

5. Duke University in South Carolina is an important center for canine research. [T / F]

6. Evan Maclean is co-director of the Canine Cognition Center at Duke. [T / F]

QUESTIONS AND ANSWERS

▶ 質問の答えを完成した後、ペアを作って、対話の練習をしてみましょう。

(1) A: How did ELTE University researchers get dogs to sit still in an MRI scanner?

   B: _____.

(2) A: What did the ELTE University researchers' results show?

   B: _____.

(3) A: How many dogs were involved in the experiments?

   B: _____.

(4) A: How does Evan Maclean evaluate the ELTE University results?

   B: _____.

SENTENCE COMPLETION

▶日本語の意味を表すように、本文から最も適当な語を選んで入れなさい。

1. 友達からのちょっとした助けでもたいていの問題を打開するのは可能だ。
   It's possible to overcome most problems (　　　) (　　) (　　　) help from your friends.

2. チンパンジーは医学的検査が行われる時に医師に協力するように訓練することができる。
   Chimpanzees can (　　　) (　　　　) (　　　) cooperate with doctors when having medical tests done.

3. 量子技術に移行することは超高速計算の新しい可能性を切り開くことになるだろう。
   Moving to quantum technology will (　　　　) up new (　　　　　) (　　　) ultra-fast computing.

4. 1997年の京都プロトコールは気候変動を遅くする試みでは重要な一歩前進だった。
   The Kyoto Protocol of 1997 was an important (　　　　) (　　　　　) in the attempt to slow climate change.

5. ウィーンやコペンハーゲンのような「スマート・シティー」は都会生活の未来を垣間見せてくれる。
   "Smart cities" such as Vienna and Copenhagen (　　　　　) (　　　) (　　　　) into the future of urban living.

SUMMARY

▶下の語群から最も適当なものを選び、要約文を完成させなさい。但し、英文の文頭に来るものは大文字にしなさい。 1-16

Many people who have a dog as a pet feel that their dog understands them, but it is difficult to know [1](　　　　　) this is really the case or just wishful thinking. Growing research evidence, though, [2](　　　　　) that dogs have much in common with humans. A team from the University of Veterinary Medicine in Vienna [3](　　　　　) that dogs could tell the difference between angry and smiling faces. In [4](　　　　　), researchers in Hungary found that dogs' [5](　　　　　) activity when listening to crying, laughing and other sounds was very [6](　　　　　) to that of humans.

> addition, demonstrated, neural, similar, suggests, whether

PRONUNCIATION

▶つなげて発音する音／つながって聞こえる音　　1-17, 18

1語1語、区切って発音するのではなく、つながるように発音します。これをマスターすると自然体で話されている英語が聞きやすくなったり、リズムで発音する時に楽に発音ができます。

次のフレーズを発音してみましょう。

in a lab environment　　[in ə] ⇒ [inə]イナ
with a little petting　　[wið ə] ⇒ [wiðə]ウィザ
lots of treats　　[lɑts ɑv] ⇒ [lɑtsəv]ロッツァヴ
were able to　　[wəːr eibl] ⇒ [wəːreibl]ワーレイブル
from whining and crying　（[ŋ] を [ŋg] で発音しないように気をつけましょう）
　　[wɑiniŋ ænd] ⇒ [wɑiniŋənd]ワイニンガンド

音声を聞いて、下線部の個所に適語を入れなさい。その後で、自分で発音してみましょう。

1. Everyone could hear the dogs ＿＿＿＿＿＿＿＿ crying.

2. Everybody ate ＿＿＿＿＿＿ cream at the birthday party.

3. I'll get by ＿＿＿＿＿ little help from my friends.

4. Fortunately, he ＿＿＿＿＿＿ to finish his work on time.

5. Sorry, ＿＿＿＿＿＿ meeting right now.

RHYTHMICAL CHANT

▶下線のところを強調しながら、リズミカルに大きな声で読みなさい。　　1-19

Hello, puppy,
What are you thinking?
Know what I'm thinking?
I bet you do.
Feeling and thinking
Like humans

自習コーナー

▶EnglishCentral にアクセスして、『見る』『学ぶ』『話す』『単語クイズ』のタスクを学習してみましょう。

UNIT 4

Gaming Online

DIALOGUE

▶空所に下の語群から適当なものを入れて、英文を完成させなさい。その後、ペアを作って対話の練習をしなさい。　1-20

A: Are you ¹(　　　　) Facebook?
B: Yes. I use it ²(　　　　) the time.
A: What do you ³(　　　　) do on there?
B: I put my photos up there and keep in ⁴(　　　　) with my friends.
　 My club also has a Facebook group.

> all,　on,　touch,　usually

VOCABULARY

▶次の語の定義を下から選びなさい。

> 1. accumulate (　)　2. virtual (　)　3. purchase (　)　4. upgrade (　)
> 5. online (　)　6. unlock (　)　7. basis (　)　8. rationale (　)

(a) replacement of an older version by a newer one, or the addition of features
(b) to gather something gradually over time
(c) an idea or situation from which something can develop
(d) to make something available for use, to open something
(e) existing on the Internet or on a computer rather than in the real world
(f) an explanation for something
(g) to buy something
(h) on the Internet or another network

19

LISTENING

▶英語を聞いて空所に適語を入れなさい。但し、カッコは内容、下線部は連音に注意しなさい。

Philip Alexiou: You know, it took radio 38 years to accumulate 50 million users. It took television 13 years; it took the Internet four years; but it took Facebook just one year to accumulate 200 million users. The media environment, to say the least, is ¹(   ) changing.

Narrator: Online social gaming like FarmVille and Mafia Wars is the second most popular online activity in the United States. ² _____ email, social networking is number one. But if you're on a social network, chances are you or one of your friends is playing games. On Facebook, 40 percent of its 500 million users today play online games.

Hundreds of millions of dollars in virtual products for social gaming will be ³(   ) in the United States in 2010. Greg Kihlström runs a web design and development firm.

Greg Kihlström: There's games that you can download free for the iPad or iPhone or, you know, things like that, but, once you download them, um, you have to, you know, in order to really unlock the ⁴ _____ ____ the game or get new ⁵(   ) or things like that, you have to purchase an upgrade.

---

to say the least
控えめに言っても

FarmVille ファームヴィル
（ゲームの名称）
Mafia Wars マフィア・ウォーズ（ゲームの名称）

chances are 多分…だ

Narrator: George Washington University's Dianne Martin says the online gaming business model is ⁶(   ), because the gaming company ⁷_____ market that is already there.

Dianne Martin: Part of their rationale for being on social media is to have this big group of friends, so you've got the friend basis and you simply use that as a platform to then do ⁸(   ) or whatever all these games are that they do.

Narrator: Greg Kihlström says, aside from being fun, another part of the genius behind a game like FarmVille, the number one Facebook game, is that people can spend a short ⁹_____ time doing simple tasks, which keeps them interested and ¹⁰(   ).

aside from 〜に加えて

TRUE OR FALSE?

▶ 内容と合っているものはTを、合っていないものはFを○で囲みなさい。

1. The Internet had about 50 million users four years after its launch. [T / F]

2. Social networking is the second most popular online activity in the United States. [T / F]

3. Forty percent of Facebook users play online games. [T / F]

4. According to Greg Kihlström, many games have a free version with paid upgrades for extra features. [T / F]

5. Dianne Martin thinks that the current business model for online gaming is a poor basis for profits. [T / F]

6. Greg Kihlström points out that top Facebook games make it easy to play in short periods of time. [T / F]

QUESTIONS AND ANSWERS

▶ 質問の答えを完成した後、ペアを作って、対話の練習をしてみましょう。

(1) A: How many users did Facebook accumulate in one year?

   B: _____.

(2) A: What is the second most popular online activity in the United States?

   B: _____.

(3) A: Who is Greg Kihlström?

   B: _____.

(4) A: Why does Dianne Martin think the business model for online gaming is good?

   B: _____.

SENTENCE COMPLETION

▶日本語の意味を表すように、本文から最も適当な語を選んで入れなさい。

1. 7時以降出かけるなら、多分時間通りにはそこに着けないだろう。
   If you leave after seven, (   ) (   ) you won't get there on time.

2. 火星探査の論拠はそこの大気が以前に地球の大気と似ていたという考えを詳細に調べることだ。
   Part of the (   ) (   ) (   ) Mars is to investigate the notion that its atmosphere used to be similar to that of earth.

3. 私は国際サッカーの試合はさておき、テレビは全く観ない。
   I never watch television, (   ) (   ) international soccer matches.

4. ハリーポッターの本は概して子供たちが最後まで読み続けるのに十分な興味を持たせ続ける。
   The Harry Potter books generally (   ) children (   ) enough to keep reading to the end.

5. レポートを書く前に、短時間でもアイデアを引き出す時間を持つ。
   Before writing a paper, I (   ) a short (   ) of time (   ) ideas.

SUMMARY

▶下の語群から最も適当なものを選び、要約文を完成させなさい。但し、英文の文頭に来るものは大文字にしなさい。 1-22

The earliest computer games from the 1950s and 1960s [1](   ) players to sit at a single computer that could not be used for anything else while the game was in [2](   ). In the 1970s, gaming on personal computers became possible, and, in the 1980s, those games started to [3](   ) graphics, which gradually became more and more [4](   ). An interesting development in the last few years is that social networking and gaming have joined together, and the online gaming [5](   ) is now said to be worth several hundreds of millions of dollars in the United States [6](   ).

> alone, incorporate, market, progress, required, sophisticated

PRONUNCIATION

▶ 日本人にとって発音や聞き取りに難しさを伴う音 [ə(:r)]　　　1-23, 24

[ə(:r)] は、アメリカ英語に特徴的な音です。(イギリス英語では、[ə:] と発音されます。)
Unit 10 の [r] の場合には、舌の真ん中を少し上げて力強く発音するのに対して、[ə(:r)] では舌の前部分に力を入れ過ぎずに発音するようにしましょう。

次の単語を発音してみましょう。

worth [wə:rθ] / work [wə:rk] / world [wə:rld] / networking [nétwə:rkiŋ] / personal [pə́:rsənl] / firm [fə:rm] / survey [sə́:rvei] / earn [ə:rn]

音声を聞いて、(　　　) 内に適語を入れなさい。その後で、自分で発音してみましょう。

1. Is the (　　　) (　　　　　) secure?

2. The (　　　　　) conducted some (　　　　　) on the (　　　　　) of all kinds of (　　　　).

3. There are millions of Facebook (　　　　) in the (　　　　).

4. The (　　　　) of the (　　　　) shakes in an (　　　　).

5. The results of a (　　　　) (　　　　) on (　　　　) are well (　　　　) reading.

RHYTHMICAL CHANT

▶ 下線のところを強調しながら、リズミカルに大きな声で読みなさい。　　1-25

Gaming on<u>line</u>
<u>Hour</u> after <u>hour</u>
Gaming a<u>lone</u> and
gaming with <u>friends</u>
<u>Hour</u> after <u>hour</u>
Even though I'm <u>tired</u>

自習コーナー

▶ EnglishCentral にアクセスして、『見る』『学ぶ』『話す』『単語クイズ』のタスクを学習してみましょう。

UNIT 5

Overtaken by China

DIALOGUE

▶空所に下の語群から適当なものを入れて、英文を完成させなさい。その後、ペアを作って対話の練習をしなさい。　1-26

A: Have you ever ¹(　　　　) to China?
B: Yes, I went to Beijing once ²(　　　　) a school trip.
A: A school trip? Wow! How was that?
B: It was really interesting. You should go ³(　　　　) if you get the chance. The ⁴(　　　　) didn't cost too much.

> flight,　been,　sometime,　on

VOCABULARY

▶次の語の定義を下から選びなさい。

> 1. decade (　) 2. manufacturing (　)　3. decline (　) 4. emergence (　)
> 5. transition (　)　　6. recession (　) 7. automobile (　)　　8. surpass (　)

(a) a reduction in the importance of something
(b) the business of producing things in factories
(c) a car
(d) a difficult time with less economic activity
(e) the process of changing from one state to another
(f) to do better than something
(g) a period of ten years
(h) becoming known or appearing

LISTENING

▶英語を聞いて空所に適語を入れなさい。但し、カッコは内容、下線部は連音に注意しなさい。

powerhouse 国を挙げて取り組んでいる国家

economic superpower 経済大国

Narrator: After more than four decades as a manufacturing and financial powerhouse, Japan's decline 1( ) China's emergence as an economic superpower. Although analysts said 2_____ a matter of time before China took the number two spot from Japan, the speed of the transition 3( ) many in Tokyo.

Woman: I knew the time would come one day, but I did not think it would be this soon.

Narrator: Analysts say China's growth played a key role in pulling the world 4_____ _____ global recession. Already this year, China has become the biggest market for automobiles—and, according to another study, the world's largest 5( ) of energy.

Lewis Cowles is senior economist of the China office of the World Bank.

Lewis Cowles: China's growth is having increasingly 6_____ on many other 7( ) of the world. In part, that is via the things that China buys: commodities, technology, capital goods from Germany, but more commodities from countries like

commodity 一次産品
（農産物や金属類など）

Australia and Brazil, many other emerging markets.

Narrator: Beijing residents expected this day would come but Victor Gao, director of China's National Association of International Studies, [8](   ) against reading too much into the latest figures.

Victor Gao: First of all, GDP is only one way to look at the economy and there is also a very important criteria*: that is the [9](   ) of the GDP. For example, when China surpasses Japan [10]_____ _____, when we look at the Japanese economy, I would personally say we still have a lot to learn from the Japanese.

National Association of International Studies
中国国际研究协会

GDP = gross domestic product 国内総生産

*正しくは criterion だが、最近では単数複数関係なく criteria を使う傾向がある。

TRUE OR FALSE?

▶ 内容と合っているものはTを、合っていないものはFを〇で囲みなさい。

1. Japan spent just under three decades as a financial powerhouse. [T / F]

2. China has become the second largest economy in the world. [T / F]

3. China became the world's largest market for automobiles. [T / F]

4. Lewis Cowles is senior economist at the Bank of China. [T / F]

5. Victor Gao is a director of China's International Association of National Studies. [T / F]

6. Victor Gao thinks China has a lot to learn from the Japanese. [T / F]

QUESTIONS AND ANSWERS

▶ 質問の答えを完成した後、ペアを作って、対話の練習をしてみましょう。

(1) A: What surprised many people in Tokyo?

　　B: _____.

(2) A: What role did China play related to a global recession?

　　B: _____.

(3) A: What kinds of things does China buy from around the world?

　　B: _____.

(4) A: What GDP-related criterion does Victor Gao point to?

　　B: _____.

SENTENCE COMPLETION

▶日本語の意味を表すように、本文から最も適当な語を選んで入れなさい。

1. 国際的な文学者としての村上春樹の出現は多くの日本人を驚かせた。
   Haruki Murakami's (   ) (   ) an international literary figure took many Japanese people by surprise.

2. 読み書きの能力は経済発展において重要な役割を果たす。
   Literacy (   ) a (   ) (   ) (   ) economic development.

3. 食事は運動選手の成績に大きな影響を与えることは現在一般的に認められている。
   It is now generally agreed that diet (   ) a major (   ) (   ) athletes' performance.

4. 多くの医師は子供たちが1日に1、2時間以上テレビを観るのを許さないよう警告する。
   Many doctors (   ) (   ) (   ) children to watch television for more than an hour or two a day.

5. イソップ物語は、人が動物から学ぶことが多いかも知れないということを示す。
   Aesop's fables show that humans may have a lot (   ) (   ) (   ) animals.

SUMMARY

▶下の語群から最も適当なものを選び、要約文を完成させなさい。但し、英文の文頭に来るものは大文字にしなさい。 1-28

Ever since the late 19th century, the United States has been the world's ¹(   ) economic leader in terms of ²(   ) GDP, while second place has changed from time to time. In the second half of the 20th century, the second-place country has been the Soviet Union, followed by Japan, and, most recently, China. The ³(   ) in positions has been due not only to China's rapid rise, but also to Japan's "lost two ⁴(   )" from 1991. China's ⁵(   ) as an economic superpower was a shock for some, but some economists point out that GDP is not everything: Japan is ⁶(   ) in many ways and China still has much to learn from Japan.

> ahead, decades, emergence, nominal, switch, undisputed

PRONUNCIATION

▶つなげて発音する音／つながって聞こえる音　　　1-29, 30

1語1語、区切って発音するのではなく、つながるように発音します。これをマスターすると自然体で話されている英語が聞きやすくなったり、リズムで発音する時に楽に発音ができます。

次のフレーズを発音してみましょう。

<u>as a</u> manufacturing and financial powerhouse　　[æz ə] ⇒ [æzə]アザ
<u>as an economic</u> superpower
　　[æz ən ekənɑmik] ⇒ [əzənekənɑmik]アザネコノミック
<u>China's emergence</u>
　　[tʃainəz imə:rdʒəns] ⇒ [tʃainəzimə:rdʒəns]チャイナズィマージェンス
analysts <u>said it</u> <u>was only</u> a <u>matter of</u> time　　[sed it] ⇒ [sedit]セディト
　　[wəz ounli] ⇒ [wəzounli]ワゾウンリ　　[mætər əv] ⇒ [mætərəv]マタラヴ

音声を聞いて、下線部の個所に適語を入れなさい。その後で、自分で発音してみましょう。

1. Haruki Murakami ＿＿＿＿＿＿＿＿ leading contender for the Nobel Prize for Literature.

2. In the 19th century, people ＿＿＿＿＿＿ wasn't possible for humans to fly.

3. Tom ＿＿＿＿＿＿＿＿＿＿ film star took many by surprise.

4. As part of my work ＿＿＿＿＿＿＿, I get to travel a lot.

5. I haven't finished yet, but ＿＿＿＿＿ a ＿＿＿＿＿ time.

RHYTHMICAL CHANT

▶下線のところを強調しながら、リズミカルに大きな声で読みなさい。　　1-31

<u>Chi</u>na's e<u>co</u>nomy?
<u>Strong</u>, strong, and <u>stron</u>ger.
If you <u>want</u> to in<u>vest</u>,
Don't <u>wait</u> any <u>long</u>er.

自習コーナー

▶EnglishCentral にアクセスして、『見る』『学ぶ』『話す』『単語クイズ』のタスクを学習してみましょう。

UNIT 6

More Salt with Your Vegetables?

DIALOGUE

▶ 空所に下の語群から適当なものを入れて、英文を完成させなさい。その後、ペアを作って対話の練習をしなさい。　1-32

A: Have you ever ¹(　　　) a kind of tomato called "shio tomato"?

B: "Show tomato"? What on ²(　　　) do you mean? I don't have a tomato to show you.

A: I said "shio tomato". "Shio" means "salt". It's a kind of tomato that is now ³(　　　) popular in Japan. It contains more salt than other kinds and is therefore sweeter and more tasty.

B: No, I don't think I've ever come ⁴(　　　) that.

> across,　earth,　quite,　tried

VOCABULARY

▶ 次の語の定義を下から選びなさい。

1. annually (　)　2. identify (　)　3. thrive (　)　4. distribution (　)
5. irrigation (　)　6. continuously (　)　7. moisture (　)　8. tolerant (　)

(a) to recognize and name something
(b) sharing things in a planned way
(c) every year
(d) without stopping
(e) able to withstand something
(f) small amounts of water present
(g) supplying crops with water
(h) become very healthy and strong

LISTENING

▶英語を聞いて空所に適語を入れなさい。但し、カッコは内容、下線部は連音に注意しなさい。

salinization 塩類化（作用）
irrigated land かんがい地
Food and Agriculture Organization 食糧農業機関

saline water 塩水、塩性水

Narrator: Salinization is ¹(   ) the world's irrigated lands by one to two percent annually, according to the U.N.'s Food and Agriculture Organization. But that doesn't faze Dutch farmer Marc Van Rijsselberghe, who has used saline water to kill some plants ²_____ identify which ones are able to thrive.

Marc Van Rijsselberghe: We put in a lot of plants in the fields and then we put them in freshwater and in seawater and all the varieties between it, and then we see which variety is ³(   ) and which variety is dying.

Free University of Amsterdam アムステルダム自由大学

Narrator: Working with scientists from the Free University of Amsterdam, Van Rijsselberghe and his team ⁴_____ farm into eight plots covered with a network of irrigation pipes. Separate pipes bring fresh and sea water to a distribution center, where a computer-controlled system ⁵(   ) irrigation water with eight different degrees of salinity.

salinity
塩分を含むこと、塩分濃度

Marc Van Rijsselberghe: And then the computer says, 'Go,' and then it goes to the fields and the dripping irrigation starts to work, and we're going to kill plants. That's it.

Narrator: Numerous sensors continuously control soil salinity and moisture. Van Rijsselberghe says they were able to harvest vegetables from ⁶_____ _____ the test plots. Although they were smaller than normal, he says they ⁷(   ) more sugar and salt, so they taste better.

Marc Van Rijsselberghe: It's a miracle. I mean, it shouldn't be a carrot. It should be dying, if we look at the data that are ⁸(   ) in the world at the moment.

Narrator: The farm managed to grow carrots, cabbage, onions, and beetroot, but potatoes proved to be the most tolerant to saline water. Van Rijsselberghe says four varieties of salt-tolerant potatoes were recently ⁹(   ) to Pakistan, where ¹⁰_____ hectares of land damaged by salinization are being prepared for testing the Dutch potatoes.

salt-tolerant 耐塩性の

hectare ヘクタール（100アール＝10000平方メートル）

TRUE OR FALSE?

▶ 内容と合っているものは T を、合っていないものは F を○で囲みなさい。

1. Salinization is leading to an annual gain of about 1–2 percent in irrigated lands. [T / F]

2. Marc Van Rijsselberghe is a scientist at the Free University of Amsterdam. [T / F]

3. The farm where Marc Van Rijsselberghe and his colleagues do their experiments is divided into eight plots. [T / F]

4. Marc Van Rijsselberghe and his colleagues were able to harvest vegetables from half of the plots. [T / F]

5. Vegetables harvested from plots with saline water tend to be smaller than normal. [T / F]

6. Marc Van Rijsselberghe is moving his farm to Pakistan. [T / F]

QUESTIONS AND ANSWERS

▶ 質問の答えを完成した後、ペアを作って、対話の練習をしてみましょう。

(1) A: How does the computer-controlled water distribution system on Van Rijsselberghe's farm work?

  B: _____.

(2) A: What do the sensors in the system do?

  B: _____.

(3) A: How do the vegetables grown in saline water taste?

  B: _____.

(4) A: What vegetable is most tolerant to saline water?

  B: _____.

SENTENCE COMPLETION

▶日本語の意味を表すように、本文から最も適当な語を選んで入れなさい。

1. 彼の収入は多くはなかったが、小さな家を買えるほどのお金をなんとか貯めることができた。
   His income was quite modest, but he (   ) (   ) save enough to buy a small house.

2. 講義はおもしろかったでしょうか。それでは、皆さんを6つのディスカッショングループに分けます。
   I hope you enjoyed the lecture. I'm now going to (   ) you (   ) six discussion groups.

3. 予防接種はいくつかの命にかかわる病気への感染を予防するとても効果的な方法であると判明している。
   Vaccination has (   ) (   ) (   ) a very effective way of preventing infection with several fatal diseases.

4. 1990年から2010年までの間に、極度の貧困の状態で生活している人々の数が約10億人減少された。
   Between 1990 and 2010, the number of people living in extreme poverty was (   ) (   ) about 1 billion.

5. 政府はホームレスの人々の数を減らすために住宅建設計画に着手した。
   The government embarked on a housebuilding program (   ) (   ) (   ) reduce the number of homeless people.

SUMMARY

▶下の語群から最も適当なものを選び、要約文を完成させなさい。但し、英文の文頭に来るものは大文字にしなさい。 1-34

The world's ¹(   ) continues to grow, which means greater demand for food. That ²(   ) has led to a series of innovations in agriculture, including the ³(   ) of new types of rice and wheat with higher yields. Another ⁴(   ) is to address the problem of land degradation, such as soil ⁵(   ) or salinization, making it possible to grow crops on land that is generally considered ⁶(   ) for agriculture.

> approach, development, erosion, increase, population, unsuitable

PRONUNCIATION

▶日本人にとって発音や聞き取りに難しさを伴う音 [v]　　CD 1-35, 36

[v] は有声の子音で、上の歯と下唇の間に摩擦や振動を感じる音です。発音するときには、上の歯を下唇に置き、その形から声を出します。Unit 12 の [f] と同じような形から生まれる音ですが、無声となります。

次の単語を発音してみましょう。

variety [vəráiəti] / vegetable [védʒtəbl] / available [əvéiləbl] / cover [kʌ́vər] / university [jùːnəvə́ːrsəti] / divide [diváid] / harvest [hɑ́ːrvist] / thrive [θraiv] / survive [səváiv] / prove [pruːv]

音声を聞いて、(　　) 内に適語を入れなさい。その後で、自分で発音してみましょう。

1. A (　　　　) of (　　　　) is (　　　　).
2. They (　　　　) the (　　　　) in the (　　　　).
3. My (　　　　) is (　　　　) into (　　　　) faculties.
4. We played (　　　　) in the (　　　　) in the (　　　　).
5. In this (　　　　) game, you can take a (　　　　) (　　　　) to (　　　　).

RHYTHMICAL CHANT

▶下線のところを強調しながら、リズミカルに大きな声で読みなさい。　　CD 1-37

Cabbages, po**ta**toes, **o**nions, and **beet**root
How will they **fare** in **sal**ty **wa**ter?
Irrigated **lands** and **sa**lini**za**tion
Losing land to **salt**, **lo**sing land to **salt**

自習コーナー

▶EnglishCentral にアクセスして、『見る』『学ぶ』『話す』『単語クイズ』のタスクを学習してみましょう。

UNIT 7

Homes for the Homeless

DIALOGUE

▶空所に下の語群から適当なものを入れて、英文を完成させなさい。その後、ペアを作って対話の練習をしなさい。　1-38

A: Have you ever ¹(　　　　) about what it would be like to be homeless?

B: No, I guess I never have. Why do you ²(　　　　)?

A: Well, after the ³(　　　　) crash of 2008, a lot of people in the U.S. lost their homes.

B: And of course there are homeless people in Japan, too. Yes, I guess it would be really ⁴(　　　　). If we ever become homeless, let's hope someone like Greg Kloehn helps us out!

A: Who?

> ask,　financial,　thought,　tough

VOCABULARY

▶次の語の定義を下から選びなさい。

1. industrial (　) 　2. tiny (　) 　3. structure (　) 　4. chilly (　)
5. protect (　) 　6. dump (　) 　7. discard (　) 　8. solar (　)

(a) something that has been built
(b) to get rid of useless materials
(c) to keep someone or something safe
(d) to get rid of something
(e) relating to industry
(f) uncomfortably cold
(g) very small
(h) related to the sun

37

LISTENING

▶ 英語を聞いて空所に適語を入れなさい。但し、カッコは内容、下線部は連音に注意しなさい。

Narrator: ¹_____ of West Oakland is dotted with tiny houses designed and built by a local artist. Greg Kloehn has built and given away at least 20 of these structures.

Greg Kloehn: I like to help them, sure. ²_____ _____ for me. I like to make things, and to do something that makes a big ³(   ) on someone's life is good.

Narrator: Oscar Young got a home and relief from chilly nights on the street.

Oscar Young: Well, it's better than living on the ground, to tell you the truth, because if it wasn't for Greg, I'd be still on the ground.

Narrator: Kloehn visits a friend called Sweetpea, who also lives in one of the houses. Inside, she is safe and can protect her ⁴(   ).
Kloehn scours the streets for construction materials, often dumped illegally at night. He brings them to his studio, where he puts the homes together.

Greg Kloehn: I mean, I've ⁵_____ _____ a building process, run out of materials, gotten in my truck, drove around to look for something;

dot ～に散在［点在・点々と存在］する、～のあちこちに存在する

scour ~ for …を探して～を調査する

that's my shopping.

Narrator: A discarded cabinet door makes a window cover. Shipping pallets become the ⁶(   ) of the structure.

shipping pallet
発送用の荷台

Greg Kloehn: Here's a pallet. The top is a door.

Narrator: The artist has ⁷(   ) a small electrical unit powered by a solar cell.

Greg Kloehn: There, I put it on a light, you know, an old lamp, so you could move it around. You can keep it optimum, just to the sun.

optimum
最適な、最善の、最も有利な

Narrator: Empty coffee bags become shingles, and a washing machine door and refrigerator ⁸(   ) become windows. Nails, screws, and glue ⁹_____ _____ together.

shingle [屋根や壁の]
こけら板、屋根板

glue 接着剤

Greg Kloehn: I kind of call them the fruits of the urban jungle. You know, here's what's dropping; here's these natural ¹⁰(   ) that we can use.

Narrator: Some on the streets once had houses of their own, but Sheila Williams has learned to live with less.

Sheila Williams: I had it all just like you people do out there, but now look at me now. I'm going to be living in one of Greg's houses, and I'm thankful to that man.

Narrator: The residents have collected discarded wood and other material for Kloehn's newest shelters.

TRUE OR FALSE?

▶内容と合っているものはTを、合っていないものはFを〇で囲みなさい。

1. Greg Kloehn has designed and built small houses and given them away.

   [T / F]

2. Kloehn has a friend called Sweetpea.   [T / F]

3. Kloehn buys his materials from a construction company.   [T / F]

4. One of the electrical units installed by Kloehn is powered by a solar cell.

   [T / F]

5. Kloehn calls the materials he finds the "vegetables of the urban jungle".

   [T / F]

6. Sheila Williams is grateful to Kloehn.   [T / F]

QUESTIONS AND ANSWERS

▶質問の答えを完成した後、ペアを作って、対話の練習をしてみましょう。

(1) A: Where does Greg Kloehn do his work?

   B: _____.

(2) A: Where does Kloehn find his construction materials?

   B: _____.

(3) A: What are some examples of materials Kloehn uses to make windows?

   B: _____.

(4) A: What have the residents been collecting for Kloehn's new shelters?

   B: _____.

SENTENCE COMPLETION

▶日本語の意味を表すように、本文から最も適当な語を選んで入れなさい。

1. もし先生方の助けがなければ、今年は卒業できないだろう。
   If ( ) ( ) ( ) my teachers' help, I wouldn't be graduating this year.

2. この薬は頭痛をすばやく取り除く。
   This drug provides quick ( ) ( ) a headache.

3. 政府の緊急経済対策は全体として経済に大きなインパクトを与えることが期待される。
   The government's stimulus package is expected to ( ) a big ( ) ( ) the economy as a whole.

4. 先生方とクラスメートたちにお世話になったことをとても感謝している。
   I'm very ( ) ( ) my teachers and classmates for all their help.

5. メルボルンは、有名な建物が点在しているが、建築に興味のある人たちにとっては素晴らしい都市だ。
   Melbourne, ( ) ( ) famous buildings, is a wonderful city for those interested in architecture.

SUMMARY

▶下の語群から最も適当なものを選び、要約文を完成させなさい。但し、英文の文頭に来るものは大文字にしなさい。 1-40

Oakland, California has drawn ¹( ) as one of the U.S.'s coolest cities, famously having the most movie theaters and ²( ) per square mile. Like most other places in the U.S., though, it was hit badly by the ³( ) crash of 2008, and there are many homeless people, especially in some ⁴( ) parts of West Oakland. Greg Kloehn is a ⁵( ) person from the area who builds makeshift homes for people from what he calls the fruits of the urban jungle—⁶( ) shipping pallets, refrigerator shelves, and so on.

> attention, creative, discarded, financial, industrial, museums

PRONUNCIATION

▶つなげて発音する音／つながって聞こえる音　　CD 1-41, 42

1語1語、区切って発音するのではなく、つながるように発音します。これをマスターすると自然体で話されている英語が聞きやすくなったり、リズムで発音する時に楽に発音ができます。

次のフレーズを発音してみましょう。

this industrial section　　[ðis indʌstriəl] ⇒ [ðisindʌstriəl]ズィシィンダストリアル
West Oakland　　[west ouklænd] ⇒ [westouklænd]ウェストウクランド
designed and built　　[dizaind ænd] ⇒ [dizaindənd]ディザインダンド
I mean it's fun for me　　[miːn its] ⇒ [miːnits]ミーニイッツ
got a home　　[gɑt ə] ⇒ [gɑtə]ガタ

音声を聞いて、下線部の個所に適語を入れなさい。その後で、自分で発音してみましょう。

1. We want to send _____ message to everyone.

2. I _____ not sure what I should do.

3. This movie was _____ directed by Woody Allen.

4. The product was faulty so we _____ refund.

5. _____ is an area of the UK that is not far from London.

RHYTHMICAL CHANT

▶下線のところを強調しながら、リズミカルに大きな声で読みなさい。　 1-43

Homes for the **homeless**,
Homes for the **homeless**,
Where should they **go**?
Where should they **go**?
Refrige**rators**, **coffee** **bags**,
The **fruits** of the **urban** **jun**gle.

自習コーナー

▶EnglishCentral にアクセスして、『見る』『学ぶ』『話す』『単語クイズ』のタスクを学習してみましょう。

UNIT 8

Care for an Exoskeleton?

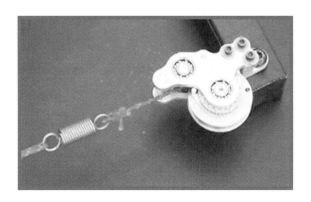

DIALOGUE

▶ 空所に下の語群から適当なものを入れて、英文を完成させなさい。その後、ペアを作って対話の練習をしなさい。　1-44

A: Have you seen *The Six Million Dollar Man*?
B: What's that?
A: It's an American TV series from the 1970s starring Lee Majors. It's about a man who ¹( ) both legs, an arm, and an eye in an ²( ), but he has them all replaced and becomes ³( ) as a result.
B: So he's a kind of ⁴( )?
A: I guess so.

> stronger,　cyborg,　loses,　accident

VOCABULARY

▶次の語の定義を下から選びなさい。

> 1. calorie ( )　2. substantial ( )　3. ankle ( )　4. spring ( )
> 5. intermittently ( )　6. catapult ( )　7. sequence ( )　8. stroke ( )

(a) a large weapon used to throw stones or other objects
(b) a unit of energy produced by food
(c) a coil that returns to its original shape after being pressed down
(d) a series of actions or other things
(e) a blockage or bursting of an artery
(f) stopping and starting often
(g) the joint between the foot and the leg
(h) a large amount or number

43

LISTENING

▶ 英語を聞いて空所に適語を入れなさい。但し、カッコは内容、下線部は連音に注意しなさい。

Narrator: Burning less calories while walking seems like a bad idea. But making the walk easier may actually get people on their ¹(   ) longer. And that, scientists say, has substantial health benefits.

Analyzing the human walk, biomedical engineers Steve(n) Collins and Greg Sawicki ²(   ) that our ankles and calves perform motions similar to a spring, coupled with a clutch that intermittently stores and releases energy. Sawicki spoke to VOA via Skype.

Greg Sawicki: We found in basic ³_____ that that system—your calf and Achilles tendon—works a lot like a catapult. So the muscle holds on to the tendon and your body actually ⁴(   ) your Achilles tendon quite a bit and ⁵_____ in the tissue and then it's given back to you to propel you forward in the world.

Narrator: Sawicki says he and his colleague Stephen Collins at Carnegie Mellon University designed a mechanical device made of carbon fiber and metal that does the same sequence of energy give-and-take outside the body. The system takes over part of the

biomedical engineer 生物医学工学者

calf ふくらはぎ

clutch クラッチ、連動機

tendon 腱

take over 〜を引き受ける、〜を引き継ぐ

work of walking and reduces the amount of ⁶(   ) energy by as much as 7 percent.

Wearing the unpowered ankle exoskeleton can help people either walk farther with the same amount of energy or restore the normal movement pattern for people who have trouble walking. Sawicki says it takes only a few minutes to get ⁷(   ) to the exoskeleton but the wearer quickly learns to tone down the muscle energy as the device takes over part of the load.

exoskeleton 外骨格

tone down 和らげる、抑える

Greg Sawicki: You really don't ⁸_____ when you take it off, and when you take it off you realize that it was there and giving you…giving you a boost.

boost [人や活動などの] 応援、後押し

Narrator: Sawicki says it is primarily intended for people recovering from surgery or a stroke, but all persons who spend a lot of time walking, such as police officers or hospital personnel, could benefit from it. At the moment, there are no plans to develop the ankle exoskeleton for the market but the ⁹(   ) say some manufacturers ¹⁰_____ interest.

TRUE OR FALSE?

▶内容と合っているものはTを、合っていないものはFを○で囲みなさい。

1. One advantage of making walking easier is that it can help people walk longer. [T / F]

2. Stephen Collins and Greg Sawicki compare walking to a spring or catapult action. [T / F]

3. The Collins and Sawicki system is a powered exoskeleton. [T / F]

4. The exoskeleton can help people restore normal walking patterns. [T / F]

5. It takes a few hours to get used to the exoskeleton. [T / F]

6. People do not notice any difference when they take off the exoskeleton. [T / F]

QUESTIONS AND ANSWERS

▶質問の答えを完成した後、ペアを作って、対話の練習をしてみましょう。

(1) A: How do Stephen Collins and Greg Sawicki view the human walk?

   B: _____.

(2) A: What is the Collins and Sawicki device made of?

   B: _____.

(3) A: How much energy can the Collins and Sawicki device save?

   B: _____.

(4) A: Who is the device intended for?

   B: _____.

SENTENCE COMPLETION

▶日本語の意味を表すように、本文から最も適当な語を選んで入れなさい。

1. 卒業して仕事を見つけた後で、仕事の生活リズムに慣れるのが難しいときがある。
   After graduating and finding a job, it is sometimes difficult to (   ) (   ) (   ) the rhythm of working life.

2. 100ヵ国以上の数百万人がマラリアに対する手ごろな治療の恩恵を受けることになるだろう。
   Millions of people in more than 100 countries would (   ) (   ) an affordable treatment for malaria.

3. 低温殺菌は元々はワインとビールの保存を目的をしていたが、今日では主に牛乳が安全に飲めるように使われる。
   Pasteurization was originally (   ) (   ) the preservation of wine and beer, but nowadays is used mainly to make milk safe to drink.

4. 住宅不足はあるが、政府にはさらに住宅を増やす計画はないようだ。
   Although there is a housing shortage, it seems that there are (   ) government (   ) (   ) build more houses.

5. 航空運賃はかなり異なっている。それで、旅行者は料金をあれこれ比べるべきだ。
   Airfares vary (   ) (   ) (   ), so travelers should shop around.

SUMMARY

▶下の語群から最も適当なものを選び、要約文を完成させなさい。但し、英文の文頭に来るものは大文字にしなさい。 1-46

The idea of ¹(   ) the human body with machine parts has long been a feature of science ²(   ) and Japanese anime—*Iron Man* and *The Ghost in the Shell* spring to mind—and has long been of ³(   ) to the military. There are also many possible ⁴(   ) uses of exoskeletons and other body enhancements. Most of these devices are powered, but a recently ⁵(   ) device from Carnegie Mellon University is unpowered, and it makes walking more ⁶(   ) through the use of a clutch and a spring.

---

announced, civilian, efficient, enhancing, fiction, interest

PRONUNCIATION

▶ 日本人にとって発音や聞き取りに難しさを伴う音 [l] 　　 CD 1-47, 48

[l] は舌の端と歯根で舌の中央に空気の閉鎖を作り、舌の両脇から空気を出すことによって生じる音です。これを発音する際には、口をわずかに開き、唇の力を抜いて発音しましょう。手で喉に触れてみると、振動を感じます。Unit 10 の [r] の発音との違いに注意して下さい。

次の単語を発音してみましょう。

like [laik] / long [lɔŋ] / load [loud] / learn [ləːrn] / lemon [lémən] / lime [laim] / lot [lɑt] / colleague [káliːg] / police [pəlíːs]

音声を聞いて、(　　) 内に適語を入れなさい。その後で、自分で発音してみましょう。

1. This (　　　　) is a (　　　　) (　　　　) than that (　　　　).
2. Don't (　　　　) (　　　　) into the (　　　　)!
3. Japan's (　　　　) expectancy is a (　　　　) (　　　　) than the (　　　　) average.
4. (　　　　) and (　　　　) are (　　　　) (　　　　) to (　　　　).
5. (　　　　) has (　　　　) about 300 (　　　　) per (　　　　).

RHYTHMICAL CHANT

▶ 下線のところを強調しながら、リズミカルに大きな声で読みなさい。　　 1-49

Exoskeletons

Making** us **stronger

Helping** us **walk

When** we are **tired

Keeping** us **going

***For** miles and miles*

自習コーナー

▶ EnglishCentral にアクセスして、『見る』『学ぶ』『話す』『単語クイズ』のタスクを学習してみましょう。

UNIT 9

Health on the Go

DIALOGUE

▶空所に下の語群から適当なものを入れて、英文を完成させなさい。その後、ペアを作って対話の練習をしなさい。 2-01

A: It seems that everything is becoming ¹(　　　　　) these days, doesn't it?
B: How do you ²(　　　　　)?
A: Well, I read somewhere that in some places where there aren't enough hospitals they have mobile ³(　　　　　) that visit villages and small towns and provide basic health care.
B: Wow, that sounds great. I'd like to find ⁴(　　　　　) more about it!

> clinics,　mean,　out,　portable

VOCABULARY

▶次の語の定義を下から選びなさい。

> 1. jostle (　) 　2. portable (　) 　3. pregnancy (　) 　4. diabetes (　)
> 5. volunteer (　) 　6. rural (　) 　7. found (　) 　8. malaria (　)

(a) to push someone in a crowd
(b) a disease carried by mosquitoes
(c) able to be moved easily
(d) a disease related to blood sugar
(e) to offer to do something without expecting money in return
(f) related to the countryside
(g) to start an organization
(h) the state of having a baby in your body

LISTENING

▶英語を聞いて空所に適語を入れなさい。但し、カッコは内容、下線部は連音に注意しなさい。

trailer [自動車に牽引される]
トレーラー

ultrasound
超音波検査 [診断]

NGO = non-governmental organization
非政府組織、民間非営利団体

mobile clinic 移動診療所

Samsung Electronics
サムスン電子（会社の名称）

specialized for ～に特化した

Narrator: These women jostling to get registered have been waiting since the early hours of the morning. This seven-meter-long trailer is a portable clinic. And for the women, it means they can get free tests and ¹(　　　　) up on their health.

In this mother-and-baby unit, women can learn their pregnancy status and have an ultrasound, ²_____ _____ getting tests for blood pressure and diabetes.

Nchaupe Mathosa is a member of a partner NGO and is volunteering today.

Nchaupe Mathosa: Most people travel, you know, miles towards the clinic or looking for assistance, so ³(　　　　) once you bring a unit like this towards the rural people, or the people who are in need, it will be very, very, very important to have it close by.

Narrator: The mobile clinic ⁴_____ by Samsung Electronics. The company has founded four solar-powered mobile clinics, each of them specialized for health needs such as eye care, dental care, or malaria ⁵(　　　　).

The solar panels, combined with battery, allow the trucks, in theory, to operate 24 hours a day.

Kea Modimoeng is Samsung Africa's Corporate Citizenship Manager.

Kea Modimoeng: In some instances, you have a clinic, which is well ⁶(   ) by an NGO, but they lack this kind of specialized services. We then ⁷_____ _____ to give it as an add-on service, which is very integral to, you know, the healthcare ⁸(   ).

Narrator: The company partners with various aid groups, universities, and local governments to know where to position its trucks. But the project is still in its infancy, and sometimes misunderstandings happen—like today, when neither Samsung nor the partner NGO brought medical gloves or stethoscopes.

Nchaupe Mathosa: The unit is quite good. It's ⁹_____ _____—it's got sonars—but some of the basic things, like gloves, and, you know, well, working material, was not actually readily ¹⁰(   ).

TRUE OR FALSE?

▶内容と合っているものはTを、合っていないものはFを○で囲みなさい。

1. At the portable clinics, women pay for health tests.   [T / F]

2. Nchaupe Mathosa works for a governmental organization.   [T / F]

3. Samsung Electronics founded 40 mobile clinics.   [T / F]

4. Kea Modimoeng works for Samsung Africa.   [T / F]

5. The mobile clinics are placed in random locations each day.   [T / F]

6. The project is now quite mature.   [T / F]

QUESTIONS AND ANSWERS

▶質問の答えを完成した後、ペアを作って、対話の練習をしてみましょう。

(1) A: What can women do in the mother-and-baby unit?

　　B: _____.

(2) A: What problem do the mobile clinics solve?

　　B: _____.

(3) A: What are some of the special health needs addressed by the mobile clinics?

　　B: _____.

(4) A: How many hours a day can the clinics operate?

　　B: _____.

SENTENCE COMPLETION

▶日本語の意味を表すように、本文から最も適当な語を選んで入れなさい。

1. 晴れた日にはいつも、数百人がアンコール・ワットで日の出を見るために朝早く集まる。
   Every fine day, hundreds of people gather in the (　　　) (　　　) of the (　　　) to see the sunrise at Angkor Wat.

2. 1時間近く待っているが、先生が私を診てくれるのはいつだろうか。
   I've (　　　) (　　　) for nearly an hour. When will a doctor be able to see me?

3. 看護師はすべての患者の様子を見るために病棟を巡回した。
   The nurse patrolled the ward to (　　　) (　　　) (　　　) all the patients.

4. その記入用紙に名前と連絡先と職業を記入して下さい。
   Please fill out the form with your name, contact details, and (　　　) (　　　).

5. 失礼ですが、お手伝いは必要でしょうか。
   Excuse me, sir, are you (　　　) (　　　) of assistance?

SUMMARY

▶下の語群から最も適当なものを選び、要約文を完成させなさい。但し、英文の文頭に来るものは大文字にしなさい。 CD 2-03

The health needs of many people in [1](　　　) parts of the world are underserved. Often, there are not enough [2](　　　) to make it economically feasible to establish a hospital, or the local economy means people do not have enough money to pay for medical services. In these cases, some form of mobile health [3](　　　) makes sense. In South Africa, mobile clinics operated by Samsung Electronics offer tests for blood pressure, diabetes, and [4](　　　) status. Each clinic also has a more [5](　　　) function, such as dental care or malaria testing. The clinics are solar-powered, meaning that they can, in [6](　　　), operate 24 hours a day.

> patients, pregnancy, provision, rural, specialized, theory

PRONUNCIATION

▶つなげて発音する音／つながって聞こえる音　　　　　　　　　　　CD 2-04, 05

1語1語、区切って発音するのではなく、つながるように発音します。これをマスターすると自然体で話されている英語が聞きやすくなったり、リズムで発音する時に楽に発音ができます。

次のフレーズを発音してみましょう。
<u>is a</u> portable clinic　　[iz ə] ⇒ [izə]イザ
<u>of a</u> partner NGO　　[ɑv ə] ⇒ [ɑvə]アバ
to <u>have it</u> close by　　[hæv it] ⇒ [hævit]ハヴィット
the mobile clinic <u>is an initiative</u>　　[iz ən iniʃətiv] ⇒ [izəniniʃətiv]イザニニシアティヴ
<u>each of</u> them　　[iːtʃ ɑv] ⇒ [iːtʃəv]イーチャヴ

音声を聞いて、下線部の個所に適語を入れなさい。その後で、自分で発音してみましょう。

1. Guam _____ in the Pacific Ocean.

2. It's sad to reach the _____ story.

3. That's _____ idea.

4. They're building a hospital down the road. It will be convenient to _____ ____ near.

5. I enjoyed _____ the books in the series.

RHYTHMICAL CHANT

▶下線のところを強調しながら、リズミカルに大きな声で読みなさい。　　　　CD 2-06

<u>Don't</u> go to the <u>doc</u>tor;
Have the <u>doc</u>tor come to <u>you</u>.
The <u>van</u> brings the <u>doc</u>tor
And the <u>doc</u>tor comes to <u>you</u>.
<u>What's</u> in the <u>van</u>? <u>What's</u> in the <u>van</u>?
Mal<u>a</u>ria <u>tes</u>ting, <u>preg</u>nancy <u>tes</u>ting,
Dia<u>be</u>tes, <u>eye</u> care, and <u>den</u>tal care, <u>too</u>!

自習コーナー

▶EnglishCentral にアクセスして、『見る』『学ぶ』『話す』『単語クイズ』のタスクを学習してみましょう。

UNIT 10 E-books Rising

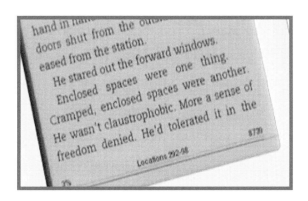

DIALOGUE

▶ 空所に下の語群から適当なものを入れて、英文を完成させなさい。その後、ペアを作って対話の練習をしなさい。　2-07

A: Do you ever buy e-books?

B: No, I ¹(　　　　) buy printed books.

A: Don't you find it ²(　　　　) to carry lots of books ³(　　　　)?

B: Well, I don't usually carry so many. And I find it easier to ⁴(　　　　) what I've read when I read a printed book.

> around,　remember,　always,　inconvenient

VOCABULARY

▶ 次の語の定義を下から選びなさい。

> 1. feature (　)　2. device (　)　3. consumer (　)　4. publisher (　)
> 5. novelist (　)　6. delivery (　)　7. retail (　)　8. means (　)

(a) a way
(b) someone who writes longform fiction
(c) a notable aspect of a product
(d) a person or company who produces books or other media
(e) distributing goods to customers
(f) a tool with specific functions
(g) someone who buys a product for their own use
(h) the sale of goods in shops to customers

LISTENING

▶ 英語を聞いて空所に適語を入れなさい。但し、カッコは内容、下線部は連音に注意しなさい。

Narrator: E-book readers are thin, like a magazine, and can store hundreds of titles on a device smaller than most paper books. They are also portable, ¹_____ _____ readers to ²(   ) books using a wireless Internet connection. Some devices even have a feature that reads the story out loud.

Sales of both e-books and digital readers are rising, as American consumers continue to ³(   ) products that fit their increasingly mobile, computerized society.

Woman: I definitely would find it more convenient for myself, if I had a whole bunch of books ⁴_____ _____ this little computer.

Narrator: Online retailer Amazon.com says it stocks more than 300,000 e-book titles. It charges about $10 each for bestsellers and new ⁵(   ) in e-book form. Hardback versions often cost much more.

Some authors and publishers have moved to digital releases to save on the cost of producing a book, such as printing, delivery, and ⁶(   ).  These costs account for more than 12 percent of the retail price of a traditional book.

Mystery novelist Debbi Mack's books are sold in electronic form. She says digital publishing is a ⁷(   ) tool for authors.

Debbi Mack: I think that, er, it provides a lot of opportunities for people to get old, out-of-print work back out on the market. If, if you can't find a publisher, and you know you have a quality product, it gives you a means of doing that.

Narrator: But critics say e-books are ⁸_____ _____ as traditional paper books. Author Eugenia Kim's new novel is available in both ⁹(   ), but she says she prefers the feel of a traditional book.

Woman 2: There's something, um, wonderful about the tactile act of turning a page, and having that whole business of having a story ¹⁰_____ as you turn a page, and I think it comes from a childhood experience with books.

tactile 触って分かる、触覚で感知できる

TRUE OR FALSE?

▶ 内容と合っているものはTを、合っていないものはFを○で囲みなさい。

1. E-book readers are thick because they contain many books. [T / F]

2. Amazon.com stocks about 3 million e-book titles. [T / F]

3. Printing, delivery, and storage account for about 12 percent of the cost of an e-book. [T / F]

4. Debbi Mack suggests that self-publishing an e-book is a good choice if an author cannot find a publisher. [T / F]

5. Eugenia Kim prefers printed books to e-books. [T / F]

QUESTIONS AND ANSWERS

▶ 質問の答えを完成した後、ペアを作って、対話の練習をしてみましょう。

(1) A: What are some advantages of e-book readers?

　　B: _____.

(2) A: Why are sales of e-books rising?

　　B: _____.

(3) A: What is an advantage of e-books for publishers?

　　B: _____.

(4) A: According to Debbi Mack, what is an advantage of e-books for authors?

　　B: _____.

Unit 10 - E-books Rising

SENTENCE COMPLETION

▶日本語の意味を表すように、本文から最も適当な語を選んで入れなさい。

1. 日本人は顆粒を摂る傾向があるが、たいていのアメリカ人は錠剤型の薬の方を好む。
   Although Japanese people tend to take granules, most Americans prefer their medicines (   ) (   ) (   ).

2. 自立学習を育成するために、学生が選択した話題を調査する多くの機会を与えるのは大切だ。
   To foster independent learning, it is important to (   ) lots of (   ) (   ) students to research a topic of their choice.

3. 平和な世界を作るために、私たちは経済摩擦を解決する手段としての戦争を放棄する必要がある。
   To create a peaceful world, we need to renounce war as a (   ) (   ) (   ) economic disputes.

4. もし海外にちょっとだけ出かけるなら、スケジュールを目的地に合わせなくても良いことが分かるかも知れない。
   If you go on a very short trip overseas, you may (   ) (   ) more (   ) not to adjust your schedule to your destination.

5. デジタル音楽が手に入りやすくなったので、多くのポピュラーのアルバムを1枚約5ドルで購入することが可能だ。
   With the increasing availability of digital music, it is possible to buy many popular albums for (   ) $5 (   ).

SUMMARY

▶下の語群から最も適当なものを選び、要約文を完成させなさい。但し、英文の文頭に来るものは大文字にしなさい。 2-09

E-books have been ¹(   ) for more than 20 years, but in their early years they were ²(   ) mainly to use on PCs, which limited their appeal. The explosion in the availability of ³(   ) devices of the last few years has meant that they are now available to almost everyone. There are cost ⁴(   ) to digital publishing, as printing is not necessary and delivery and ⁵(   ) are much easier. But it is thought that printed books and e-books will continue to ⁶(   ) for a long time.

---
advantages, around, coexist, mobile, restricted, storage

PRONUNCIATION

▶ 日本人にとって発音や聞き取りに難しさを伴う音 [r]　　　2-10, 11

[r] は舌の端が歯根に接近することで作られる隙間から生じる音です。[r] の音を出す前に「ウ」と発音するときのように口を突き出しましょう。特に間違えやすいのは、[l] の発音です。[r] と [l] の発音の違いに注意してください。

次の単語を発音してみましょう。
rise [raiz] / reader [ríːdər] / release [rilíːs] / retail [ríːteil] / American [əmérican] / computerized [kəmpjúːtəraizd] / print [print] / electronic [ilèktránik]

音声を聞いて、(　　　) 内に適語を入れなさい。その後で、自分で発音してみましょう。

1. Are there any (　　　　　) in the (　　　　　)?
2. Let's be (　　　　) about the (　　　　　) for the (　　　　) industry.
3. Some (　　　　) (　　　　) to (　　　) papers in (　　　　) (　　　　) than (　　　　) form.
4. Many universities have (　　　　) (　　　　　) their (　　　　) systems.
5. This (　　　　) has (　　　) (　　　　　) (　　　　　).

RHYTHMICAL CHANT

▶ 下線のところを強調しながら、リズミカルに大きな声で読みなさい。　　2-12

<u>E</u>-books, <u>E</u>-books every<u>where</u>

On <u>phones</u> and <u>tablets</u> and <u>e</u>-book <u>readers</u>,

<u>Hundreds</u> of <u>books</u> on a <u>tiny</u> de<u>vice</u>.

<u>Reading</u> on <u>it</u> is <u>very</u> <u>nice</u>.

<u>Read</u> and <u>read</u> and <u>read</u> again

On the <u>tram</u>, on the <u>train</u>,

On the <u>bus</u>, on the <u>plane</u>.

自習コーナー

▶ EnglishCentral にアクセスして、『見る』『学ぶ』『話す』『単語クイズ』のタスクを学習してみましょう。

UNIT 11

Health in the Forest

DIALOGUE

▶空所に下の語群から適当なものを入れて、英文を完成させなさい。その後、ペアを作って対話の練習をしなさい。　2-13

A: Do you like herbal medicines?
B: Herbal medicines? What kinds of things do you have in ¹(　　　)?
A: Well, when you have a ²(　　　), do you take "kakkon-tou"?
B: Oh, I ³(　　　) I do take kakkon-tou. But that's about ⁴(　　　).

　　　　　all,　cold,　guess,　mind

VOCABULARY

▶次の語の定義を下から選びなさい。

1. graveyard (　)　2. traditional (　)　3. transfer (　)　4. income (　)
5. arrest (　)　6. weigh (　)　7. extract (　)　8. certify (　)

(a) to measure weight
(b) an area of land where things are buried
(c) money earned from work
(d) to state officially that something is true or genuine
(e) following ideas or using things that have existed for a long time
(f) to take someone to a police station or prison
(g) to move from one place to another
(h) to remove a substance

61

LISTENING

▶ 英語を聞いて空所に適語を入れなさい。但し、カッコは内容、下線部は連音に注意しなさい。

Narrator: ¹_____ increasingly common ²(　　　) in Kenya: graveyards of what once were mighty forests, teeming with life. The Kakamega Forest in Western Kenya is one of the country's last ³(　　　　　) stands. Plants in the forest are being damaged or killed because people harvest them for traditional medicines.

So, to save Kakamega Forest, an international research group has transferred two popular plants out of the forest and into ⁴_____ farmers such as Mary Shimuli. Shimuli grows a half-acre's ⁵(　　　　) of Ocimum kilimandscharicum and harvests the plant every six months. She says that, besides saving the forest, her harvests bring her family a better income.

Mary Shimuli: I used to go to the forest for ⁶(　　　　　) but I was afraid of being arrested. After I realized that the project is fruitful for me, I stopped going to the forest. I ⁷(　　　　　) to buy two cows.

---

mighty 広大な

teem with 〜で満ちあふれている

stand 木立、群生

ocimum kilimandscharicum オシマム・キリマンシャリカム（植物の名称）アフリカに自生する青いバジル

fruitful 有意義な、有益な

Narrator: Shimuli and other farmers bring what they harvest to a nearby factory ⁸_____ by the community and supported by African Insect Science for Food and Health or ICIPE. The ocimum is weighed, dried, then processed. The oil ⁹(_____) is used to manufacture Naturub, a balm and an ointment used to treat flu, cold, chest congestion, aches, pain and insect bites. The products have been ¹⁰_____ _____ by the government.

ICIPE = International Centre of Insect Physiology and Ecology
国際昆虫生理生態センター
Naturub ナチュラブ（薬の名称）
balm 鎮静薬
ointment 軟膏
flu インフルエンザ
congestion うっ血

TRUE OR FALSE?

▶ 内容と合っているものはTを、合っていないものはFを○で囲みなさい。

1. Mary Shimuli is a member of an international research group.　　[T / F]

2. Shimuli harvests Ocimum kilimandscharicum every six months.　　[T / F]

3. Shimuli's income has improved since she started harvesting ocimum.　[T / F]

4. Shimuli has bought two horses.　　[T / F]

5. The factory that processes the ocimum is supported by ICIPE.　　[T / F]

6. Naturub is used to treat pain.　　[T / F]

QUESTIONS AND ANSWERS

▶ 質問の答えを完成した後、ペアを作って、対話の練習をしてみましょう。

(1) A: Why are plants in the Kakamega Forest being damaged?

　　B: _____.

(2) A: What has the international research group done to save Kakamega Forest?

　　B: _____.

(3) A: What was Shimuli afraid of when she went to the forest?

　　B: _____.

(4) A: What is the plant used for?

　　B: _____.

SENTENCE COMPLETION

▶日本語の意味を表すように、本文から最も適当な語を選んで入れなさい。

1. 会社のホームページを運営することに加えて、この仕事は私たちのコンピュータの安全を確認することを必要とする。
   (   ) (   ) the company website, this job entails checking the security of our computers.

2. 多くの人が家庭で地震やその他の災害に備えて2週間分の食料を蓄えておくようアドバイスする。
   Many people advise families to store two (   ) (   ) (   ) food in case of earthquake or other disaster.

3. かつて、私は溺れるのが怖かったので泳ぐのが嫌いだった。
   I used to hate swimming because I was (   ) (   ) drowning.

4. 午後5時に会社をなんとか出ることができれば、コンサートに間に合う。
   I'll be on time for the concert as long as I (   ) (   ) get out of the office at 5 p.m.

5. 食物アレルギーは最近ますます一般的になっているようだ。
   Food allergies appear to be becoming (   ) (   ) these days.

SUMMARY

▶下の語群から最も適当なものを選び、要約文を完成させなさい。但し、英文の文頭に来るものは大文字にしなさい。 CD 2-15

Most herbs come from ¹(   ) forests, and deforestation is leading to a concern that ²(   ) of these herbs could be threatened—not to mention the possibility that many unresearched herbs could become ³(   ) before there is a chance to analyze them chemically and establish any health benefits. One forest that is ⁴(   ) threatened is the Kakamega Forest in Kenya. There, an international research group has ⁵(   ) two species of medicinal herb out of the forest for farmers to grow and ⁶(   ).

> extinct, harvest, severely, supplies, transferred, tropical

PRONUNCIATION

▶つなげて発音する音／つながって聞こえる音   2-16, 17

1語1語、区切って発音するのではなく、つながるように発音します。これをマスターすると自然体で話されている英語が聞きやすくなったり、リズムで発音する時に楽に発音ができます。

次のフレーズを発音してみましょう。

<u>one of</u> the country's last remaining stands　　[wʌn ɑv] ⇒ [wʌnəv]ワンナヴ

<u>damaged or</u> killed　　[dæmidʒd ɔr] ⇒ [dæmidʒdɔr]ダミジィドア

<u>an international</u> research group　　[ən intərnæʃnl] ⇒ [ənintərnæʃnl]アニンタナシャナル

<u>out of</u> the forest　　[aut ɑv] ⇒ [autəv]アウタヴ

<u>such as</u> Mary　　[sʌtʃ æz] ⇒ [sʌtʃəz]サチャズ

音声を聞いて、下線部の個所に適語を入れなさい。その後で、自分で発音してみましょう。

1. Households headed by children are ＿＿＿＿＿＿＿＿ common sight in sub-Saharan Africa.

2. Monaco is ＿＿＿＿＿＿ the world's most densely populated countries.

3. A good thing to get before going overseas ＿＿＿＿＿＿＿＿＿＿ driver's license.

4. Many were ＿＿＿＿＿＿＿ killed in the battle.

5. Basic items ＿＿＿＿＿＿＿ kettle and a bottle of water are provided.

RHYTHMICAL CHANT

▶下線のところを強調しながら、リズミカルに大きな声で読みなさい。　2-18

<u>Ka</u>kamega <u>Fo</u>rest, <u>Ka</u>kamega <u>Fo</u>rest

A<u>mong</u> the <u>last</u> forests <u>left</u> in <u>Ken</u>ya

<u>O</u>cimum, a<u>ca</u>cia, and <u>bi</u>tter alo<u>e</u>

A <u>trea</u>sure trove of <u>pre</u>cious, me<u>di</u>cinal <u>herbs</u>

<u>Ho</u>neybush, <u>roo</u>ibos, and <u>peri</u>winkle

<u>A</u>frican <u>trea</u>sures for our <u>health</u>

自習コーナー

▶EnglishCentral にアクセスして、『見る』『学ぶ』『話す』『単語クイズ』のタスクを学習してみましょう。

UNIT 12

Gravity-defying Skateboards

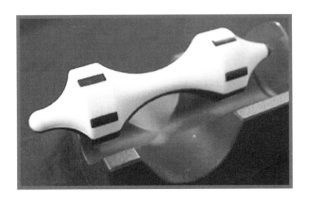

DIALOGUE

▶ 空所に下の語群から適当なものを入れて、英文を完成させなさい。その後、ペアを作って対話の練習をしなさい。　2-19

A: Have you ¹(　　　　) tried skateboarding?
B: Yes, I did it a ²(　　　　) times when I was in high school. It's really difficult!
A: You can say that ³(　　　　). I tried it yesterday and I couldn't keep my ⁴(　　　　) at all.

> again,　balance,　ever,　few

VOCABULARY

▶ 次の語の定義を下から選びなさい。

> 1. magnet (　) 　 2. principle (　) 　 3. hover (　) 　 4. earthquake (　)
> 5. proof (　) 　 6. metal (　) 　 7. surface (　) 　 8. response (　)

(a) the basic idea that a system is based on
(b) the top layer of an object
(c) to stay a short distance above the ground or other surface
(d) a piece of metal that attracts other metal
(e) something that is done in reaction to something else
(f) a hard, usually shiny, substance
(g) facts that demonstrate something is true
(h) a sudden shaking of the earth's surface

LISTENING

▶ 英語を聞いて空所に適語を入れなさい。但し、カッコは内容、下線部は連音に注意しなさい。

repulsion 反発

counteract
［～の力に］反対に作用する

levitate 空中浮揚する

maglev train
リニアモーターカー、
磁気浮上式の鉄道車両

turn on ～を作動させる

Narrator: It's easy to see that mutual repulsion between the same poles of two magnets can counteract the force of ¹(   ) and make an object levitate or hover in space, like this magnetic toy.

Since the 1980s, that principle has ² _____ _____ in so-called maglev trains in Europe, Japan, and China, that hover above the track. With no ³(   ) between the carriage and the surface, and hence no friction, maglev trains are almost ⁴(   ) and can move very fast.

Architect Greg Henderson, who founded the company Arx Pax with his wife, Jill, says the same technology can make anything hover, even buildings.

Greg Henderson: Imagine that there's an earthquake, and the early-warning system turns on the hover systems, and the supports ⁵_____ as the building starts to hover. The shaking stops, the supports return, and no-one in that room or that building ever knew there was an earthquake.

Narrator: As a proof of the ⁶(   ), Henderson's company created the first maglev hoverboard, called Hendo, ⁷(   ) of holding a single person about 2.5 centimeters above a metal surface.

Greg Henderson: We are creating a magnetic field and then, through ⁸_____ induction—that's part of our secret sauce—we're creating a secondary and equal magnetic field in this conductive surface.

induction 誘導

conductive 伝導性のある

Narrator: For now, batteries that power Hendo's four engines ⁹(   ) only for a short time, but design engineer Kyle O'Neil says for experienced skateboarders it is enough to learn how to control the hoverboard.

Kyle O'Neil: Some people say it's like snowboarding; some people say, you know, this is like how I imagine a hoverboard is supposed to be, which is ¹⁰_____ _____ response, because it's…no-one's ever ridden one before.

TRUE OR FALSE?

▶内容と合っているものはTを、合っていないものはFを○で囲みなさい。

1. A maglev train is quiet because there is no contact between the train and the surface. [T / F]

2. The maglev principle is useful only in transportation. [T / F]

3. Greg Henderson's wife is called Gill. [T / F]

4. Hendo can hold several people about 2.5 cm above a metal surface. [T / F]

5. Hendo has four engines. [T / F]

6. Hendo is battery-powered. [T / F]

QUESTIONS AND ANSWERS

▶質問の答えを完成した後、ペアを作って、対話の練習をしてみましょう。

(1) A: What is the principle behind maglev trains?

    B: _____.

(2) A: What is Arx Pax?

    B: _____.

(3) A: How would the system work with a building in the event of an earthquake?

    B: _____.

(4) A: How do people describe the hoverboard?

    B: _____.

SENTENCE COMPLETION

▶ 日本語の意味を表すように、本文から最も適当な語を選んで入れなさい。

1. 参加型の方法で最も学習する人たちは運動学習者と呼ばれる。
   People who learn best (　　　　) a hands-on (　　　　) are called kinesthetic learners.

2. 私立の小学校の校長は物語を話すことに重点的に取り組むことが秘訣であると言った。
   The head of a private elementary school said that a focus on storytelling was the school's (　　　　) (　　　　).

3. コンピュータサイエンスでは、1バイトとはxやeのような単一文字を持つことができる記憶容量の単位である。
   In computer science, a byte is a unit of storage (　　　　) (　　　　) holding a single character, such as x or e.

4. あたりを見回して下さい。そうすれば、スマートフォンが今ではほとんどいたるところに存在するのを知るのは容易だ。
   Look around you, and it's (　　　) (　　　) (　　　) that smartphones are now nearly ubiquitous.

5. 煉瓦が羽根よりも早く落ちるようにするのは煉瓦の方がより密度が高いからである。
   It is the greater density of a brick that (　　　　) it (　　　　) faster than a feather.

SUMMARY

▶ 下の語群から最も適当なものを選び、要約文を完成させなさい。但し、英文の文頭に来るものは大文字にしなさい。　2-21

Operating according to the same ¹(　　　　) as a maglev train, hoverboards, those futuristic devices seen in *Back to the Future*, are now becoming a ²(　　　　). The owner of a company that makes hoverboards says that they are just a ³(　　　　) of concept, and that he hopes that his Arx Pax ⁴(　　　　) will be adopted much more widely, for example to protect buildings in case of an ⁵(　　　　), or in vacuum cleaners in the clean rooms used to make electronic ⁶(　　　　).

> earthquake, components, principle, proof, reality, technology

PRONUNCIATION

▶ 日本人にとって発音や聞き取りに難しさを伴う音 [f]　　　　　2-22, 23

[f] は無声の子音です。上の歯を下唇に当てながら、その間を息が出るように発音しましょう。但し、上の歯と下唇の接触がしっかりできていない場合、ちゃんとした摩擦音が出せないので注意しましょう。[v] の発音との違いに注意してください。

次の単語を発音してみましょう。
found [faund] / fast [fæst] / fall [fɔːl] / field [fiːld] / defy [difái] / before [bifɔ́ːr] / proof [pruːf] / if [if] / few [fjuː] / perform [pərfɔ́ːrm]

音声を聞いて、(　　　　) 内に適語を入れなさい。その後で、自分で発音してみましょう。

1. Do you (　　　　) meat or (　　　　)?
2. His (　　　　) has lived a (　　　　) (　　　　).
3. The tragedy (　　　　) him with (　　　　).
4. He (　　　　) (　　　　) what he was looking (　　　　).
5. He went to (　　　　) with his (　　　　) to see the (　　　　) Tower.

RHYTHMICAL CHANT

▶ 下線のところを強調しながら、リズミカルに大きな声で読みなさい。　　　　2-24

A: What's *that* in the *air*?

B: It's a *skate*board, a *skate*board.

A: A *skate*board?

B: *Well*, a *ho*ver*board*.

A: A *ho*ver*board*?

B: *Yes*, that's *right*. It *uses maglev tech*.

A: *Maglev tech*?

B: *Yes*, that's *right*. It's *Back* to the *Future* right *now*!

自習コーナー

▶ EnglishCentral にアクセスして、『見る』『学ぶ』『話す』『単語クイズ』のタスクを学習してみましょう。

UNIT 13
Living Your High-tech Dreams

DIALOGUE

▶ 空所に下の語群から適当なものを入れて、英文を完成させなさい。その後、ペアを作って対話の練習をしなさい。 2-25

A: Hey, do you have a 3-D printer?

B: What are you ¹(　　　　　) about this time?

A: Well, I've been doing a science project, and I have a ²(　　　　　) a world-shattering invention may be just around the ³(　　　　　).

B: Well, let me know if you get ⁴(　　　　　), and I'll see what I can do.

> anywhere,　corner,　feeling,　on

VOCABULARY

▶ 次の語の定義を下から選びなさい。

> 1. assist (　)　　2. invention (　)　　3. encourage (　)　　4. equipment (　)
> 5. textiles (　)　　6. fee (　)　　7. motto (　)　　8. leap (　)

(a) money that you pay for a service
(b) to help someone
(c) a short phrase summarizing the goals of an institution
(d) the tools and other items needed for a job
(e) a big jump
(f) to give someone the courage or means to do something
(g) something original that has been designed or made
(h) woven cloth made in large quantities

LISTENING

▶英語を聞いて空所に適語を入れなさい。但し、カッコは内容、下線部は連音に注意しなさい。

2-26

CNC router = computerized numerical controlled router コンピュータ数値制御ルータ
prototype 試作品

Narrator: Retired lawyer Maurice Mountain is using a CNC router to produce a prototype of his Presto Emergency Boat Ladder. He's planning to mass-produce his invention, a small [1](   ) ladder that can be clipped on the side of a boat to assist people who fall into the water.

innovation 革新、刷新、イノベーション

Maurice Mountain: I [2]_____ innovation. I think people who probably have had ideas rolling around in the back of their minds for years but never have had the [3](   ) to actually put them into production or even experiment with them would find this place wonderful.

high-tech 先端技術の

Narrator: The place that Mountain is [4](   ) to is TechShop, a studio that makes high-tech equipment available to its members.

do-it-yourself 日曜大工
fabrication 製作、製造

Isabella Musachio: So TechShop is a do-it-yourself maker space and fabrication studio. So, as you can see, when you come in, we have all these different areas of  the shop, and we have a metal shop, wood shop, plastics lab, lasers, 3-D printers, electronics, textiles. I mean, we have so many different areas and we have all this equipment that is available to anybody above the age

laser レーザー（光線）
electronics 電子機器

of ⁵_____.

Narrator: At TechShop, with membership fees starting at just over $100 per month, members have ⁶(   ) to million-dollar equipment, 3-D modeling, laser cutters, and water jets—all at their fingertips.

Isabella Musachio: Our motto is 'build your dreams here' because you can really come in with ⁷_____, and then, with the help of TechShop, make that leap from an idea to building your project or your prototype, or even your business.

Narrator: One example is Square, which came out of the TechShop ⁸(   ) in San Francisco. Now, Square is used to charge about $8.8 billion in transactions every year.

The consumers of products that were ⁹_____ TechShop even include President Obama, who thinks innovation is the first step to the future and that TechShop is giving ¹⁰(   ) people the tools they need to turn their ideas into reality.

President Obama: Because of advances in technology, part of the opportunity is now to make the tools that are needed for production, and prototypes are now democratized. They're in the hands of anybody who's got a good idea.

at one's fingertips
指先にある、すぐ手に届くところにある、すぐ使えるようにしてある

democratize 民主化する

TRUE OR FALSE?

▶ 内容と合っているものは T を、合っていないものは F を○で囲みなさい。

1. Maurice Mountain is a busy lawyer. [T / F]

2. TechShop is available to adults only. [T / F]

3. TechShop's motto is "Build your dreams here." [T / F]

4. The principle of TechShop is that you bring a prototype and pay for TechShop to manufacture it. [T / F]

5. Square paid TechShop $8.8 billion to make its equipment. [T / F]

6. President Obama thinks TechShop is a good idea. [T / F]

QUESTIONS AND ANSWERS

▶ 質問の答えを完成した後、ペアを作って、対話の練習をしてみましょう。

(1) A: What is Maurice Mountain's invention?

   B: _____.

(2) A: What is TechShop?

   B: _____.

(3) A: What facilities are available at TechShop?

   B: _____.

(4) A: What is TechShop's motto?

   B: _____.

SENTENCE COMPLETION

▶日本語の意味を表すように、本文から最も適当な語を選んで入れなさい。

1. 人は訪問するにはお金がかかる所としてヨーロッパを見る傾向がある。しかし、もし時期をうまく選べば、航空運賃は400ドルからある。

   People tend to see Europe as an expensive place to visit, but, if you choose your time well, airfares (　　　) (　　　) around $400.

2. 「品質第一」はここABCエンタープライズのモットーです。

   "Quality first" is (　　　) (　　　　) here at ABC Enterprises.

3. ソフトウェア会社は私たちのコンピュータをより安全にするために多くのことができるが、結局のところは、安全確保はユーザーの手中にある。

   Software companies can do many things to make our computers more secure but in the final analysis security is (　　　) (　　　) (　　　) of users.

4. 失敗は成功への第一歩であると時々言われる。

   It is sometimes said that failure is the (　　　) (　　　) (　　　) success.

5. 1950年代に、ウォルト・ディズニー・カンパニーは映画製作からディズニーランドのようなテーマパークの運営へと急成長した。

   In the 1950s, the Walt Disney Company made (　　　) (　　　) (　　　) making movies to operating theme parks such as Disneyland.

SUMMARY

▶下の語群から最も適当なものを選び、要約文を完成させなさい。但し、英文の文頭に来るものは大文字にしなさい。　2-27

One thing that can lead to a stronger manufacturing [1](　　　　) is new inventions to manufacture. Inventions have until now been difficult to bring to [2](　　　　) because of cost: tools are expensive, as are the software programs used to [3](　　　　) new products. This situation is beginning to change, though, as [4](　　　　) workshops with a wide range of advanced tools and [5](　　　　) are set up around the U.S. and [6](　　　　).

> design, fruition, low-cost, materials, overseas, sector

PRONUNCIATION

▶つなげて発音する音／つながって聞こえる音 　　　　　　　　2-28, 29

1語1語、区切って発音するのではなく、つながるように発音します。これをマスターすると自然体で話されている英語が聞きやすくなったり、リズムで発音する時に楽に発音ができます。

次のフレーズを発音してみましょう。

<u>is using a</u> CNC router　（[ŋ] を [ŋg] で発音しないように気をつけましょう）
　　[iz juːziŋ ə] ⇒ [izjuːziŋə]イジュージィンガ

<u>produce a</u> prototype　　[prəduːs ə] ⇒ [prəduːsə]プロデューサ

<u>his invitation</u>　　[hiz inviteiʃən] ⇒ [hizinviteiʃən]ヒズィンビテイション

<u>fall into</u> the water　　[fɔːl intə] ⇒ [fɔːlintə]フォーリンタ

I <u>think it encourages</u>
　　[θiŋk it enkəːridʒəz] ⇒ [θiŋkitenkəːridʒəz]シィンキテンカーリジズ

音声を聞いて、下線部の個所に適語を入れなさい。その後で、自分で発音してみましょう。

1. That's important information. I _____ young people.

2. Be careful not to _____ the wall!

3. Next, _____ carrot and add it to the soup.

4. I greatly admire _____.

5. I'm _____ version of the software.

RHYTHMICAL CHANT

▶下線のところを強調しながら、リズミカルに大きな声で読みなさい。　　2-30

<u>Tech</u>Shop, <u>Tech</u>Shop,

<u>Living</u> your <u>high</u>-tech <u>dreams</u>

<u>Tech</u>Shop, <u>Tech</u>Shop,

<u>Build</u> your <u>dreams</u> <u>here</u>

<u>Tech</u>Shop, <u>Tech</u>Shop,

The <u>first</u> step <u>to</u> the <u>future</u>

自習コーナー

▶EnglishCentral にアクセスして、『見る』『学ぶ』『話す』『単語クイズ』のタスクを学習してみましょう。

UNIT 14

Onward to Jupiter

DIALOGUE

▶ 空所に下の語群から適当なものを入れて、英文を完成させなさい。その後、ペアを作って対話の練習をしなさい。　2-31

A: Do you think humans will live on other ¹(   ) in the future?
B: Well, it doesn't seem very ²(   ).
A: Why ³(   )?
B: The ⁴(   ) on most planets isn't suitable for humans.
A: Mmm, I guess you're right, but it's nice to dream!

> environment,　likely,　not,　planets

VOCABULARY

▶ 次の語の定義を下から選びなさい。

1. core ( )　2. composition ( )　3. evolve ( )　4. gravity ( )
5. instrument ( )　6. massive ( )　7. polar ( )　8. radiation ( )

(a) a force that pulls small things towards larger things
(b) the parts of something and how they are put together
(c) the central part of something
(d) a device used to do a specific task, such as measuring something
(e) energy, for example nuclear, from a specific source
(f) very big indeed
(g) to gradually change and develop
(h) concerning the most northern or southern part of a planet, etc.

LISTENING

▶英語を聞いて空所に適語を入れなさい。但し、カッコは内容、下線部は連音に注意しなさい。

2-32

lurk 潜む
NASA アメリカ航空宇宙局

Narrator: What lurks beneath the planet Jupiter's cloud cover? Scientists hope to find out when NASA's Juno spacecraft begins its one-year ¹(　　　　) of the massive planet. Juno project manager, Jan Chodas...

Jan Chodas: So here I have a model of the Juno Spacecraft. The core structure contains our propulsion tanks and most of the instruments are mounted on the ²_____ aft decks. But obviously, the dominant ³(　　　　) here are the large solar arrays.

propulsion 推進させること

aft 船尾（の方）にある
solar arrays 太陽光線を集まるためのアンテナ

Narrator: Juno's wings are covered in solar cells. And the craft will rely on solar energy as it ⁴(　　　　) through space for the next five years.

At its ⁵_____ to Jupiter, Juno will be about 5,000 kilometers above the cloud tops and it will dip down below the planet's dangerous radiation belts. Juno will spend a year in polar orbit and its eight instruments will study Jupiter's magnetic and gravity fields, as well as the composition of the planet's ⁶(　　　　　　) and core. NASA scientists say this information will help them answer key questions about the way Jupiter and the solar system evolved.

dip 急に高度を下げる
polar orbit 極軌道

Chodas ⁷_____ to explain the

beginning of Juno's 640-million kilometer track from NASA's Kennedy Space Center to the colossal planet.

colossal 巨大な

Jan Chodas: Shortly after launch, about five minutes, we start the solar array deploy sequence. There go the arrays. It should take probably about one to three minutes to get the arrays out. And then, if we are left at an ⁸(   ) that is not directly sun-pointed, we will turn to within 20 degrees of the sun to illuminate the arrays and start recharging the battery. And that will be ⁹_____ our way to Jupiter…

deploy 展開する

illuminate ～に光を当てる
recharge
［蓄電池に］再充電する

Narrator: … and possibly bringing us ¹⁰(   ) to a better understanding of the universe, once Juno reaches Jupiter in 2016.

TRUE OR FALSE?

▶ 内容と合っているものはTを、合っていないものはFを○で囲みなさい。

1. Scientists don't expect to find out anything about Jupiter.　　[T / F]

2. Juno will orbit Jupiter for five years.　　[T / F]

3. Juno will be powered by solar energy.　　[T / F]

4. Juno has 18 instruments.　　[T / F]

5. Juno's trip to Jupiter will be about 640,000,000 kilometers.　　[T / F]

6. Juno will reach Jupiter in 2060.　　[T / F]

QUESTIONS AND ANSWERS

▶ 質問の答えを完成した後、ペアを作って、対話の練習をしてみましょう。

(1) A: What is Juno?

　　B: _____.

(2) A: How close will Juno get to Jupiter?

　　B: _____.

(3) A: What will Juno's instruments study?

　　B: _____.

(4) A: How will the information from Juno help us?

　　B: _____.

Unit 14 - Onward to Jupiter

SENTENCE COMPLETION

▶日本語の意味を表すように、本文から最も適当な語を選んで入れなさい。

1. チームの最後の勝利はタイトルへより近づけることになる。
   The team's latest victory (   ) it (   ) to the title.

2. 一国の経済がもっぱら観光産業に依存するのは良いことではない。
   It is not good for a country's economy to (   ) solely (   ) tourism.

3. 昼食直前に企画会議を開きましょう。
   Let's have a planning meeting (   ) (   ) lunch.

4. カナダは世界で2番目に広い国だが、カナダ人の約75パーセントがアメリカ国境から100マイル以内に住む。
   Canada is the second largest country in the world but around 75 percent of Canadians live (   ) 100 miles of the U.S. border.

5. 私の本がついに出版されることになり私はとてもうれしい。10年近く前に書き始めた。
   I'm so happy that my book has finally been published; I (   ) (   ) it nearly ten years.

SUMMARY

▶下の語群から最も適当なものを選び、要約文を完成させなさい。但し、英文の文頭に来るものは大文字にしなさい。 2-33

Until now, most of the information we have on Jupiter comes from flyby ¹(   ) starting in the 1970s. The best-known of these are the Voyager ²(   ) that approached Jupiter in 1979, discovering Jupiter's ring and finding out many details of Jupiter's moons. The Galileo was the first ³(   ) to orbit Jupiter, doing so for more than seven years starting in 1995. The Galileo found ammonia clouds in Jupiter's atmosphere and learned much about the planet's magnetosphere. Juno, ⁴(   ) in 2011, will spend a year in polar orbit of Jupiter, getting more ⁵(   ) information on the planet's magnetic and gravity fields, as well as on the ⁶(   ) of its atmosphere and core.

composition, detailed, launched, missions, probes, spacecraft

PRONUNCIATION

▶日本人にとって発音や聞き取りに難しさを伴う音 [w] は有声の子音です。これを発音するときに、歯が唇に触れないようにして、唇を丸めて音を出しましょう。母音のような発音にならないように注意しましょう。違う子音で始まる韻をふむような音節を言った後に練習すると簡単です。

2-34, 35

次の単語を発音してみましょう。

ten [ten] - men [men] - when [wen] / sing [siŋ] - ring [riŋ] - wing [wiŋ] /
Bill [bil] - hill [hil] - will [wil] / pull [pul] - bull [bul] - wool [wul] /
sigh [sai] - buy [bai] - why [wai]

音声を聞いて、(　　　) 内に適語を入れなさい。その後で、自分で発音してみましょう。

1. (　　　) are (　　　) going on (　　　)?
2. (　　　) have (　　　) stopped before arriving at (　　　)?
3. (　　　) do you (　　　) to (　　　) a movie?
4. Many people (　　　) to know (　　　) (　　　) is a country.
5. I (　　　) if it (　　　) be (　　　) today.

RHYTHMICAL CHANT

▶下線のところを強調しながら、リズミカルに大きな声で読みなさい。

2-36

A: <u>Where</u> are you <u>going</u>, <u>Juno</u>, <u>Juno</u>?
B: I'm <u>going</u> <u>into</u> <u>space</u>.
　 I'm <u>leaving</u> for <u>Jupiter</u> and <u>visiting</u> its <u>moons</u>:
　 Ca<u>llis</u>to, <u>Ganymede</u>, Eu<u>ropa</u>, and <u>Io</u>.
A: <u>How</u> will you <u>get</u> there, <u>Juno</u>, <u>Juno</u>?
B: I'm <u>going</u> to use the <u>power</u> of the <u>sun</u>.
　 <u>So</u>lar <u>power</u> is the <u>way</u> to <u>go</u>
　 And <u>using</u> solar <u>power</u> is <u>lots</u> of <u>fun</u>.

自習コーナー

▶EnglishCentral にアクセスして、『見る』『学ぶ』『話す』『単語クイズ』のタスクを学習してみましょう。

EnglishCentral

UNIT 15

Pumpkins at Halloween

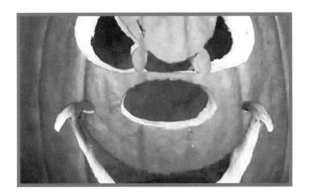

DIALOGUE

▶ 空所に下の語群から適当なものを入れて、英文を完成させなさい。その後、ペアを作って対話の練習をしなさい。　2-37

A: Hey, do you want to go grape ¹(　　　　) this weekend?

B: Is it that ²(　　　　) already? Sure. Do you know a good place?

A: Yeah. It's about 30 minutes outside the city. The ³(　　　　) is that I don't have any transportation.

B: Oh, I ⁴(　　　　) it. Let's go in my car then.

> get,　picking,　trouble,　season

VOCABULARY

▶ 次の語の定義を下から選びなさい。

| 1. wander (　) | 2. perfect (　) | 3. vine (　) | 4. decorate (　) |
| 5. hectare (　) | 6. generation (　) | 7. treat (　) | 8. porch (　) |

(a) the members of a family of about the same age
(b) not having any faults
(c) to make something look more attractive
(d) a structure built onto the entrance of a house
(e) something special
(f) a plant with long, thin stems
(g) a unit of area, 10,000 m²
(h) to walk around without a clear purpose

LISTENING

▶英語を聞いて空所に適語を入れなさい。但し、カッコは内容、下線部は連音に注意しなさい。

Narrator: The Huffer Family Farm is a busy place each October, as families wander through the six-hectare Jumbo's Pumpkin Patch, ¹(   ) for the perfect pumpkin.

Sarah Cosgrove: It's a good one; I think it's looking good.

Narrator: Sarah Cosgrove has been coming to Jumbo's for several years with her husband and two sons.

Sarah Cosgrove: The landscape is really pretty and we usually are able to get our pumpkins ²_____ _____ the vine. We'll carve them up and put them  on our front porch to decorate our house.

Narrator: The Huffer family has ³(   ) these 53 hectares near Maryland's Catoctin Mountains for more than 140 years. David Huffer and his brother are the seventh generation to run the farm, with help from their families. The pumpkin patch was opened in 1994, and Huffer says it's a ⁴(   ) to see pumpkins on the vine instead of in a grocery store.

David Huffer: A lot of kids don't realize how pumpkins grow. They're having fun and learning ⁵_____ _____ the same time.

25 **Narrator:** Other fun activities ⁶(   ) taking pony rides and eating ice cream. Rodney Kline, a friend of Huffer's, churns the home-made treat in an ice cream maker connected to an old gas engine from 1918.

Rodney Kline: Back in the day, the farmer would have used
30 it to run, like, a small corn grinder or corn sheller, maybe the well pump.

Narrator: Huffer says families also enjoy the hayride that
35 brings them to the pumpkin patch.

David Huffer: We have people who just like to ride the wagons because that's all they ⁷(   ) to do. They just like to ⁸_____ and they'll do that all afternoon, which is fine, and they have a good
40 time doing it, so….

Narrator: Diane Wilkerson is amused watching her ⁹(   ) search for pumpkins.

Diane Wilkerson: Especially when they try to ¹⁰_____ _____, and then they go to the ground
45 when they find out that they're too heavy.

TRUE OR FALSE?

▶ 内容と合っているものはTを、合っていないものはFを○で囲みなさい。

1. The Huffer Family Farm tends to be busy in October. [T / F]

2. The Huffer family has had the farm for 53 years. [T / F]

3. The pumpkin patch was opened in 2004. [T / F]

4. For some children, visiting the farm is their first chance to see how pumpkins grow. [T / F]

5. Rodney Kline made the ice cream maker in 1918. [T / F]

6. Some people like to ride the wagons all afternoon. [T / F]

QUESTIONS AND ANSWERS

▶ 質問の答えを完成した後、ペアを作って、対話の練習をしてみましょう。

(1) A: How long has the Cosgrove family been going to the Huffer Family Farm?

　　B: _____.

(2) A: Where is the Huffer Family Farm?

　　B: _____.

(3) A: What can people do at the Huffer Family Farm?

　　B: _____.

(4) A: Who is Rodney Kline?

　　B: _____.

Unit 15 - Pumpkins at Halloween

SENTENCE COMPLETION

▶日本語の意味を表すように、本文から最も適当な語を選んで入れなさい。

1. 健康がどんなに大切であるのを悟るのは病気の時だけだ。

   It is only when we are sick that we (　　　) (　　　) precious health is.

2. 私は疲れきっている。したいのはただ家にいて休憩することだけだ。

   I'm exhausted, and staying at home to rest is (　　) (　　) (　　) to do.

3. 洪水の被災者たちは政府からの経済的支援によって立ち直った。

   The victims of the flood got back on their feet (　　　) financial (　　　) (　　　) the government.

4. 体の具合が良くないときには、働き過ぎて回復が遅くなるリスクを冒す代わりに家にいて回復する方が良いかも知れない。

   When you're not feeling well, it may be better to stay home and recover (　　　) (　　) (　　　) too hard and risking a slower recovery.

5. 英語が急に上手くなる学生の多くが用いる方略には、毎日語彙の勉強することもある。

   The strategies used by many students who make rapid progress in English (　　　) (　　　) vocabulary every day.

SUMMARY

▶下の語群から最も適当なものを選び、要約文を完成させなさい。但し、英文の文頭に来るものは大文字にしなさい。　CD 2-39

For those of us who are not able to grow our own fruits and ¹(　　　　　), going to a farm and picking some ourselves is an enjoyable activity that ²(　　　　　) our links with the land. The U.S. has many "pick your own" farms. The crops available ³(　　　　　) widely. Maryland is a state with an especially wide selection, including ⁴(　　　　　), blackberries, eggplants and Asian pears. Perhaps most popular, though, are pumpkin farms, with ⁵(　　　　　) families wanting to pick one for Halloween. Families can spend an ⁶(　　　　　) day or half-day at the farm.

> broccoli, countless, enjoyable, strengthens, vary, vegetables

PRONUNCIATION

▶つなげて発音する音／つながって聞こえる音　　　　　　　　2-40, 41

1語1語、区切って発音するのではなく、つながるように発音します。これをマスターすると自然体で話されている英語が聞きやすくなったり、リズムで発音する時に楽に発音ができます。

次のフレーズを発音してみましょう。

right off the vine　　[rait ɔf] ⇒ [raitɔf]ライトフ
carve them up　　[ðem ʌp] ⇒ [ðeməp]ゼマップ
put them on our front porch　　[ðem ɔn auər] ⇒ [ðemənauər]ゼモナウア
learning something at the same time　　[sʌmθiŋ æt] ⇒ [sʌmθiŋət]サムシィンガット
in an ice cream maker　　[in ən ais] ⇒ [inənais]イナナイス

音声を聞いて、下線部の個所に適語を入れなさい。その後で、自分で発音してみましょう。

1. Let's do some exercises _____ getting up.

2. Oh, you dropped your books. Let me help you pick _____.

3. Here are my things. Could you put _____ box?

4. I found _____ the library.

5. He found himself _____ rock _____ hard place.

RHYTHMICAL CHANT

▶下線のところを強調しながら、リズミカルに大きな声で読みなさい。　　2-42

Happy Hallo<u>ween</u>, Happy Hallo<u>ween</u>,
<u>Wit</u>ches and <u>ghouls</u> and <u>spoo</u>ky <u>screams</u>,
<u>Bon</u>fires, <u>apple</u> bobbing,
<u>Trick</u> or <u>treat</u>.
Let's <u>go</u> and pick a <u>pump</u>kin
for the <u>jack</u>-o'-lantern <u>scene</u>.

自習コーナー

▶EnglishCentral にアクセスして、『見る』『学ぶ』『話す』『単語クイズ』のタスクを学習してみましょう。

TEXT PRODUCTION STAFF

| edited by | 編集 |
| Eiichi Tamura | 田村 栄一 |

| English-language editing by | 英文校閲 |
| Bill Benfield | ビル・ベンフィールド |

| cover design by | 表紙デザイン |
| SEIN | ザイン |

CD PRODUCTION STAFF

narrated by	吹き込み者
Josh Keller (AmE)	ジョシュ・ケラー（アメリカ英語）
Edith Kayumi (AmE)	イーディス・カユミ（アメリカ英語）

VOA News Plus
見て学ぶVOAニュース

2016年1月20日　初版発行
2023年9月5日　第8刷発行

編著者　安浪　誠祐
　　　　Richard. S. Lavin

発行者　佐野 英一郎

発行所　株式会社 成 美 堂
　　　　〒101-0052東京都千代田区神田小川町3-22
　　　　TEL 03-3291-2261　FAX 03-3293-5490
　　　　https://www.seibido.co.jp

印刷・製本　倉敷印刷（株）

ISBN 978-4-7919-4794-2　　　　Printed in Japan

・落丁・乱丁本はお取り替えします。
・本書の無断複写は、著作権上の例外を除き著作権侵害となります。